CHILD

OF THE

BLITZ

For
Hugh

with best wishes

Ken Blasbery

Published by   Ken Blasbery
                        10 Aster Crescent, Runcorn WA7 3HS
                        Tel. 01928 712050

In association with Northern Publishing Service

Distributed by   Northern Publishing Service
                        28 Bedford Road
                        Firswood
                        Manchester M16 0JA
                        Tel. 0161 862 9399

ISBN: 1 899181 40 7

Copies can be obtained from the author or
the distributor at above addresses.

Printed in 12/14pt Times New Roman.

Printed by   MFP Design & Print
                        Longford Trading Estate
                        Thomas Street
                        Stretford
                        Manchester M32 0JT
                        Tel. 0161 864 4540

FOREWORD

This book is the result of hearing a conversation on Radio Merseyside between Billy Butler and Wally Scott, who had just interviewed three ladies who had been teenagers during the War. They had been recounting their experiences at work and at home, when Billy said to Wally, "What a pity there are no accounts of what it was like to be a school child at that time", to which Wally agreed.

This conversation set me thinking of my experiences and the result is this account of life during the period September 1939 to August 1945.

ACKNOWLEDGEMENT

To Miss E.R. Newton, Head Teacher of Dovecot County Primary School, for her help and encouragement in the writing of this book, and for the use of the Junior School Log Book from which I was able to refresh my memory of the early days of the war.

To the staff of the Reference Department of the Central Library, William Brown Street, Liverpool, for their help in tracing the Log Book of the former senior school which closed in 1966. This school changed name three times during the period 1966-1990, and was finally found under the name of Yewtree Comprehensive.

To my wife, Olwen, for her help in the original typesetting of the manuscript.

Also, to Suzanne and Mark of PC Hire, Warrington for their help in the final typesetting.

Finally to Doreen Mallandaine, Managing Director of North West Auto Trader and Ken Olsen, Production Controller, for allowing me to use their full production facilities for the make up of these pages.

ABOUT THE AUTHOR

Now retired after over 50 years in the Printing Industry, he lives in Runcorn with his wife, Olwen.

He spends time as a Dysphasic Support Volunteer, part of the Stroke Association.

He is also studying at Halton College of Further Eduction for a B.S. Initial Certificate in Teaching. His aim is to help students' read and write English as a second language. A life-long member of the Boys' Brigade, he is also a Steward of Frodsham Methodist Church.

DEDICATION

*This book is dedicated to the memory of the children of
Liverpool who lost their lives during the aerial
bombardment of the City.*

May this dreadful act never be repeated.

Contents

1939

The Day War Broke Out!

IT'S WAR!... We had just listened to our Prime Minister, Neville Chamberlain, say on the radio, "This morning, the British Ambassador in Berlin handed to the German Government a final note stating that, unless we heard from them by eleven o'clock that they were prepared at once to withdraw their troops from Poland, a state of War would exist between us. I have to tell you now that no such undertaking has been received, and that consequently this country is at War with Germany".

"We" were the Blasbery family. Dad, Charles Herbert, known to my mother's family as "Charlie", and to his family as "Sam". Mother, Alice, me, Kenneth Charles and my younger brother, Vernon.

We lived at No. 4 Ashover Avenue, Liverpool 14. Dad and mum were both thirty seven years old, I was nine and Vernon was eight.

We had listened to the Prime Minister's speech on our new 'Ultra' electric radio. After the broadcast, dad went out into our back garden. He had seen one of our neighbours, Mr. Reidy, in his garden. He had married a German lady after the end of the first War in 1919. I went out to join dad, who was in earnest conversation with Mr Reidy, who had tears in his eyes and was saying "What if the authorities come and take her away? What will I do?" I remember dad saying "They know that Mrs Reidy is a naturalised British Citizen and I am sure they will not take her away". This seemed to calm Mr Reidy down and they continued

1

their conversation whilst I wandered off to play. This day was Sunday, 3rd September, 1939.

Our house was the middle one of a block of three. We lived close to the corner of East Prescot Road, and from our front door we could look to Page Moss Avenue tram terminus. From this vantage point we could see the trams leaving the terminus and when dad or mum wanted to catch one, they could walk over the road to the tram stop. This was excellent in the winter, as there were no shelters provided for waiting passengers.

As a nine-year old, hearing about the 'Clouds of War' mentioned in many of the news broadcasts, I had often looked at the sky and wondered which clouds would bring the War.

Just before the declaration of War, we had been on holiday to the Isle of Man for two weeks. On Saturday 1st September, we were coming home from Douglas on the mid-day ferry. We boarded the boat called the *King Orry* and settled down for the voyage home. Normally this voyage took about four hours, but on this occasion, it took eight hours, due, we were told, to the possibility of German spies being on board, spying on any passing warships.

We had been staying in the Port of Peel, on the West Coast, at the home of Mr and Mrs McMeekin in Rake Lane, close to the harbour. Dad knew Mr McMeekin, who worked for the Isle of Man Steam Packet Company, from his work with Shell Mex. & B.P. Ltd., where he worked at Dingle Oil Terminal, as a Clerk, dealing with the many shipping companies in the Port of Liverpool.

We had a wonderful time playing on the beach with Orry and Roy, the sons of the McMeekins. We would go to the breakwater below Peel Castle to see the fishing fleet as they arrived early in the morning, and again at night when they set sail for the fishing grounds.

Dad had been a member of the Royal Air Force for seven years, just after the end of the first War. He served in Iraq, being stationed near Basra, and in Bombay, India. He had been back in

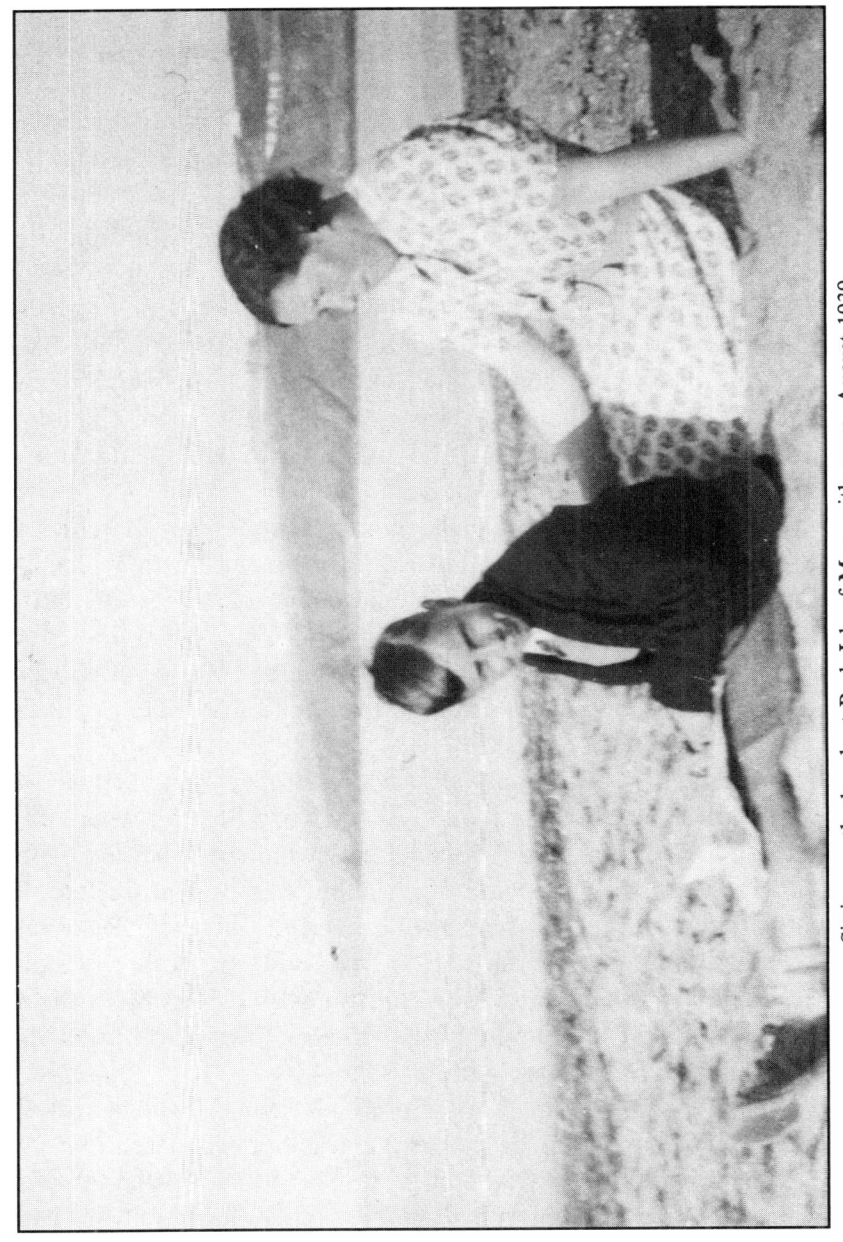

Sitting on the beach at Peel, Isle of Man, with mum, August 1939.

civilian life for eleven years, but considered himself fit to return to the service. One night, a high-ranking officer came to our house, he had come to offer dad an immediate promotion to the rank of Sergeant, if he would return to duty. I think he was keen to go, but mum and his employers had other ideas, so he did not go, remaining at home to play his part in the War effort.

Across the City on Sunday 3rd September, many children were preparing to be evacuated to safer areas of the country. Megan and Olwen Pritchard, living at 14 Freshfield Road, Liverpool 15, with their widowed mother, Margaret, packed their small bags and reported to their school. The Morrison Primary, in Greenbank Road, at 12 noon. There they were each given a bar of chocolate and a tin of corned beef. All the children had labels attached to their coats to ease identification.

After a tearful farewell, the whole school was marched to Sefton Park Station to board a train to Flint in North Wales. At that time the parents had no idea where their children were being taken.

On arrival, they were taken to a hall, where they were `chosen' by a Mrs Jones, herself a mother of many children. She took them to Bagillt, where she lived.

My cousins, John and Philip Spratt, of Alderson Road, Liverpool 15 also reported to Lawrence Road School, where they had the same treatment as Megan and Olwen before setting off by train for Tattonhall, near Chester. Another cousin, Harold Temple, who was just turned five years old, lived in Salisbury Road. He was too young to be evacuated, so stayed with his mother. His dad was in the Merchant Navy, working for Alfred Holt & Co. Ltd., sailing with the Blue Funnel Line to the Far East. Harold was also a pupil at Lawrence Road infants School.

My only girl cousin, Betty Spratt, lived at 57 Cairns Street, Liverpool 8. Betty like Vernon and I, was not evacuated.

Megan and Olwen arrived at the Jones' home, given a meal of toasted cheese, then put to bed with the other children. Miss Bell, the head teacher of the Morrison School, was in charge of the

4

Children from Lawrence Road School who were evacuated to Tattenhall, near Chester, October 1939.

evacuation party. The girls were sent to school in Greenfield. Discipline was strict, the evacuees were told by Miss Bell that if they went to the local cinema to see the Alfred Hitchcock thriller 'Dial M for Murder' they would be sent home. Needless to say they all went to see it. Unfortunately, nobody was sent home.

The parents of the evacuated children were eventually informed of the addresses of the people who now had temporary charge of their children. Mrs Pritchard made regular weekend visits to Bagillt. On one occasion, whilst giving the girls a close examination of their hair, she found that Megan's head was infested with Lice. She immediately packed their things and returned to Liverpool.

Meanwhile, on that first night of War, I went to bed wondering when there would be any fighting. We had our Gas Masks, and very soon would have identity Cards, showing your name, address and you identity number. Mine was NICU84/3.

On the radio at the beginning of the War, we had for weekend listening, programmes such as:- in the Canteen, Band Wagon, with Richard Murdoch and Arthur Askey, the Sunday Orchestral concert, and Scrap Book for 1906.

Sam Costa gave songs at the piano and there was a talk by the American broadcaster, Raymond Gram Swing. The News would be followed by official and other announcements.

Monday the 4th September, brought the official closure of all places of public entertainment until Friday the 15th when cinemas and other places of entertainment were reopened.

Dad was now employed by the Ministry of Fuel & Power, doing the same job, but now in an official capacity. He was appointed Chief Bunkering Officer, which meant he was responsible for the supply and delivery of all types of oil to ships arriving and departing from the Mersey.

To enable him to carry out his duties, a telephone was installed in our dining room. It was a very heavy black instrument. To make a call, the receiver was lifted to your ear, and then there was a wait until the operator at the telephone exchange would ask

"Number Please", after giving the number there would be a short wait until the operator came back with "You're through now", and you could start your conversation. Our number was Stoneycroft 1731. We had this phone for some time, until one night dad wanted to speak to the Captain of a vessel about to sail from Gladstone Dock. He waited for the operator to answer him for almost fifteen minutes. When she did talk to him she was very indignant, and told him that "There is a War on you know". Very soon after this episode we were given a new telephone with a dial facility that enabled dad to make his own calls.

He had to go to Convoy briefings so that he could arrange the necessary delivery of oil to the ships. These briefings would take place at the Royal Liver Buildings at the Pier Head, where the Royal Navy had their headquarters.

We were given an Anderson Shelter to erect in our back garden. This entailed digging a hole about four feet deep by about eight feet long so that the corrugated sheets of metal could be positioned partly below ground. The soil taken from the hole was then piled over the metal to give greater protection in the event of a bomb blast. However, where we had dug our hole, there was an underground stream, so the hole quickly filled with water. The Council sent workmen to dig another hole nearer to the house. Then they cemented a concrete tank into the bottom of the hole and installed four bunks for our comfort. We used the shelter when the weather was warm, but dad converted our inside coalplace under the stairs so that we could remain warm and safe.

To further protect our homes, our parents were given instructions on various ways of preventing damaged, such as putting sticky tape over the windows to prevent glass splinters causing injuries if there was an explosion. Blackout curtains and blinds were made to prevent any light shining up into the sky and assisting an enemy aircraft find its position.

Shortly after the start of the war, two wrecked motor cars were positioned one on each side of our Avenue as a road block. All the local boys and girls had a wonderful time playing on them. One day an old man, wearing a black overcoat and black hat came along, he asked us a lot of questions about the two cars. We gave a few answers and ran home to our mums. We decided that he was a spy, but I suppose he was just and interested old man.

Before the start of the war, our school had been closed to allow the teachers to make plans for the evacuation of the school. Some young children and their mothers were evacuated on the 4th of September to Rhyl and Abergele.

The submarine *Thetis* was opened on the 7th September to reveal the body of a sailor. She sank in Liverpool Bay on 4th June, 1939 whilst on trials from Cammel Laird's shipyard, Birkenhead. There were 70 fatalities on board. Dad was to have gone as a representative of his company, but he was called away at the last moment on other urgent business.

During the first few months of the war over 3,000 children and mothers were evacuated to the Chester area from Liverpool, but by the end of October, 1,250 had returned to their homes.

All schools were now closed by order of the Board of Education, on 25th September. We were notified that we would be put into groups to be taught in various places. My group was to meet in the vestry of the church of the Holy Spirit, Dovecot. There we would be given work to be completed at home, by Mr Hughes, one of the teachers. He would arrive on his bicycle, give a few instructions, then pedal away to another group. I also went to the home of one of my friends, Alfie Forfar, for more work. The Education Committee paid 3d per household per session towards the cost of heating and lighting the houses used to give out work.

The Battleship H.M.S. *Royal Oak* was torpedoed at her home base at Scapa Flow on 16th October. This came as a great shock to me, as dad had taken me not too many months previously on board her when she was in the Gladstone Dock. I felt very proud standing on top of her main gun turret, and to think that she was now below the water without having had the chance to fight, was very upsetting.

As the months passed, very little seemed to be happening, except for the gradual disappearance from the streets and shops of little things, such as the 'Walls Ice cream man' on his dark blue tricycle with the words 'Stop me and buy one', painted on the front. One used to be at the school gate at home time in the afternoon. Snofruits were the favourite at 1d each, but if you only had a half-penny, he would cut one in half.

Outside Dovecot Library, there would stand a West Indian man selling Cinder Toffee. He would be there every Friday night and on Saturday morning when the Granada Cinema had the childrens' morning show. Then one day he did not appear, and was gone for ever.

We had a set of cigarette cards issued by the Wills Tobacco Company, depicting Air Raid Precautions. On these cards there were illustrations on one side and useful information on the other, such as:- The Stirrup Pump, which was to be used on small fires, started by incenciary bombs. This pump would be used by one person who could both pump the handle and direct to stream of water on to the fire. Another card was of an Anti-aircraft Gun mounted on a mobile platform. This was a three inch gun which could fire a shell of 16lb weight up to 20,000 feet in twenty three seconds, and could fire up to twenty rounds per minute.

The Government was very worried about children in the danger areas. Lord De La Warr, President of the Board of Education said ``We cannot afford to, as a Nation let three quarters of a million children grow up as little Barbarians, and the Government has no intention of doing so. The situation is under almost daily revue".

A curfew was imposed on the opening of shops. They would close at 6pm. on five days and 7pm. on one day. Lighting restrictions were placed on shops at the same time, and customers were advised to shop early. Books, magazines and comics were in the shops and among the popular editions were the Dandy, Beano, Radio Fun, and the Boy's Own Paper. This publication would print fantastic stories of daring and heroism plus humorous jokes

9

of the time. It was a monthly publication and cost 6d.

In the Liverpool Echo on Saturdays, there would be Auntie Muriel's Treasure Chest especially written for children. For the grownups, especially the ladies there were the Picturegoer at 3d, Film Pictorial, and Cinegram Preview at 2d to name but a few. There was also Woman's World, Home Companion and Home Notes priced at 3d, 3d, and 2d.

The Radio Doctor broadcast after the 8a.m. news every morning, giving advice and new ways of doing almost everything, including tripe! S.P.B. Mais gave regular talks on how to cope with limited supplies of all commodities.

At Christmas, Vernon and I were taken to the Pavilion Theatre, Lodge Lane to see Arthur Lucan and Kitty McShane in the pantomime 'The Old Woman Who Lived in a Shoe'. To get there, we travelled by the number 10B tram to Kensington, where we transferred to the 26 tram to Lodge Lane. After the show, we went to our grandparents home in Moss Grove, where we had supper. Our journey home was by way of the 60 bus that ran from Lark Lane to Seaforth. We alighted at Old Swan, where we again boarded the 10B tram from home.

On Christmas morning Vernon and I woke to find we had Hornby Train sets. Mine was a goods set with an oval track, whilst his was a passenger set with a circular track. There were other accessories such as bridges and signals. We also received gifts of books, and the traditional orange, apple and some nuts. For Christmas dinner, we had a huge Goose, which mum had prepared the night before and had been cooking slowly overnight, served with roast and boiled potatoes, sprouts, carrots and turnip, topped off with home-made stuffing and gravy. After this feast, we had Christmas pudding and white sauce.

It was about this time that the Ministry of Food was asking housewives to register with a Grocer and a Butcher, as food rationing was to start early in 1940.

We were encouraged to listen to the news bulletins and to read the newspaper. The Liverpool Echo was delivered every night and we would read about the fighting in France and Finland.

The favourite songs at the end of 1939 were: 'We're Gonna Hang out the Washing on the Siegfried Line', and 'Over the Rainbow'. British films showing were: 'Goodbye Mr Chips', and 'The Hunchback of Notre Dame', starring Charles Laughton.

1940

Digging for Victory

Food became the main concern of our mothers at this time, with the introduction of rationing on 8th January. Tea, sugar, cream, butter, meat and petrol were the first items. Our weekly rations varied according to supply, but the lowest amounts were: bacon and ham, 4 oz., sugar 8 oz., tea 2 oz. Meat was based on price at 1/10d, butter 2 oz., cheese 1 oz., margarine 4 oz., cooking fat 2 oz., Soap was also rationed, hard soap 4 oz., toilet soap or flakes 3 oz,. soap powder 6 oz, soft soap 6 oz.

We returned to as near as possible schooling early in January. I was in the `A' stream and went into Class 4. We had regular Air Raid drills where we would go to the air raid shelters on the playing field, that had been built whilst the school was closed. The head master would blow a whistle, and we would go as quickly as possible to our designated shelter which had the class number painted on the door. The register would be called to account for us all, and we would be led by the teacher in singing songs such as `Run Rabbit Run'.

When the drill was completed to the satisfaction of the Head, we would return to our classroom and resume our lessons. Our head master was Mr E.J. Griffiths and some of the teachers I remember were Miss Mann, a matronly lady with white hair and gold rimmed spectacles. She always wore a green overall. Miss Price, who was from the West Indies, Mr Colquohoun, Mr Hughes, Miss Hughes, Mr Dutton, Mr Phumphrey, Miss Sexton and Miss Charlton.

We were encouraged to grow our own food. This was taken up at home and later at school, where each class was given a piece of land to cultivate. Our school efforts went to Alder Hey, and Broadgreen Hospitals. Harvest festival gifts went to sick pupils and elderly neighbours of the school. Vegetables were also sent to Westminster House.

Our back garden was very big, so we turned the bottom end into a vegetable plot. We grew potatoes, carrots, turnips, beetroot, cabbage, onions, lettuce, rhubarb, raspberries and strawberries.

January saw the beginning of the worst winter on record. The Isle of Man ferry, *Rushen Castle* took three days to complete a normal four hour crossing from Douglas to Liverpool. A tender had to be sent out to the Bar Lightship to deliver fresh water and food to the ship.

We had a front garden which was bordered by a privet hedge, which had grown to a height of about 3'6". When the snow began to fall, and the wind blew, the garden soon filled up to the top of the hedge with snow. It was a beautiful sight, but very cold. Transport had great difficulty in operating. There were no Crosville buses to Prescot, and the trams ran when and where they could. At one time, only about 25% of public transport was operating.

There was a story of one tram load of passengers staying on the vehicle for ten hours because the snow was so deep they were unable or unwilling to get off!. A train on the Cheshire Lines railway travelling between Liverpool and Manchester was `lost' for three days, and had to be dug out by soliders. The Thames froze over on 17th January, for the first time since 1888. Further storms swept over the country on the 27th.

On the radio we tuned in each weekday for Children's Hour, introduced by Derek McCulloch. He had been badly wounded as a boy soldier in the Great War, being left for dead on the Somme battlefield. He survived to become known to all children as 'Uncle Mac'. He always ended the programme with 'goodnight

Ruth Bassnett *(far right, front row)* with friends from Pheobe-Ann Street, going to Sunday School, 1940.

14

children ... everywhere'. Another favourite was the 'Romany' programmes. Our 'radio aunties', Doris and Muriel, would go into the country with 'Romany' and his dog Rak. We would learn about the habits of the Fox, Badger and other woodland creatures.

Dad and mum sometimes tuned in to 'Lord Haw Haw' as we called him. His real name was William Joyce, and he broadcast from Germany. He had a nasal twang and used such phrases as 'Old chap' and 'Honest Injun', which his German script writers believed were used by the average British worker. He was captured at the end of the war, trying to escape into Denmark. He was tried, found guilty of treason, and hanged.

School work continued as normally as possible, but the severe weather, and the shortage of fuel to heat the school was apparent. The classroom temperature was only a little over 36 degrees fahrenheit, and we had to wear our coats and mackintoshes to keep warm.

The supply of milk at school continued and we were able to have our bottles in the morning and afternoon, provided it was paid for. From memory it was half-penny a bottle.

In February, the Government launched an Anti-gossip Campaign. Posters and Newspaper advertisements appeared with such slogans as 'Careless talk costs lives', Be like dad, keep mum', 'Walls have ears' and 'keep it dark'.

On 12th February there were 399 boys on roll, 263 of them could get home within five minutes of an Air Raid Warning siren sounding during school time. The co-operation of parents was sought, and if a senior member of a family was away from home during the day, boys who lived more than five minutes away from their homes could stay with their friends. A rehearsal took place on the 26th, followed later in the week by sending home two classes at a time, care being taken to avoid congestion when leaving the school entrance in Stonefield Road.

Dad came home one night early in March, to tell us that the lined *"Queen Elizabeth"* had arrived safely in New York.

Our school gardening sessions started again after the winter

Ruth Bassnett *(with Union Jack shield, front row)*, May Day 1940.

months. Great pride was felt when we saw the first little shoots of our vegetables push through the soil.

As Vernon and I were nine and ten years old, we would go for our monthly haircut by ourselves. There was a Barbers' shop about 200 yards from home, on Liverpool Road, at the corner of Dinas Lane. This was owned by Mr Tom Ford, he had a brother Jim, who had been called up to serve in the Royal Air Force. When he was come on leave, he would assist in the shop. If the boys were small there would be a plank of wood placed across the arms of the chair to sit on. Those boys big enough, would stand holding the back of the chair, with their chin in the head rest whilst their hair was cut. A boy's haircut cost 6d.

Next door to Ford's was the local Fish and Chip shop. We didn't have many meals of fish and chips, but when we did, I would be sent to the shop. There was always a long queue, and it was not uncommon to wait for upwards of an hour before being served. There was a man in charge of the frying range, and two or three women constantly making chips and serving the queue. There was a mirror over the cooking range, but it was always covered in condensation from the boiling fat below. The walls were of white tiles, and these too were running in condensation. When it came close to your turn to be served, one of the women would ask what you wanted. When the order was taken, the fish would be dipped in batter, and placed in the fat to cook. the chips were constantly cooking, so there was no need to order them.

Chips were sold at 4d or 6d per portion, with fish cakes at 3d. Mushy peas were 2d a portion, and the fish was 6d and 9d. There was always salt and vinegar available on the counter, which was to be used according to each individual taste.

In America and other Empire countries, steps were being taken to provide British children with foster homes. 'The Richest Woman in the World' Mrs Doris Duke Cromwell offered $250,000 a year to take 500 children to America and support them. Ten thousand families in the U.S.A. were offering homes, as were 500 private schools and other organisations, with a waiting list for 5,000 more. One New York woman said 'I have eight, and one on the way, but I can make room for one of these poor little things'. An English Peer offered to pay the fares of 500 children to go to Australia. Families there were offering homes for 18,000 children. The Government agreed to extend the limit of 5,000 it had agreed with the Australian authorities.

The first batch of 71 children arrived in New York on July 8th and a further 80 were disembarked in Halifax Nova Scotia from the liner *Sythia*.

On the food front, it was decided to standardise a loaf of bread. There had been forty five different loaves in England and eighty five in Scotland and these were reduced to four.

A Liverpool schoolgirl, Meryl Reed, of Rodney Street, was on her way to American foster parents, when the ship she was a passenger in was torpedoed and sank in the Atlantic Ocean. After many hours in an open boat, she was eventually rescued and returned to Liverpool.

Another young girl, Pamela Weeks aged eight, launched the 'Pamela Spitfire Fund'. Early in July, the Liverpool Education Committee discussed the imposition of a curfew on children in the city. Alderman Hogan said "It is very desirable to include secondary and elementary children in this curfew". However it was never implemented.

Another item for discussion at this time was a request for advice from the foster parents of those children evacuated to North Wales. These parents wanted permission to whip children in their care who were disobedient. The Education Committee decided there was no code to be followed and no decision was made.

The 'Five Minute Warning' for boys to go home when the siren sounded was tested on 15th July when a warning was sounded at 13.20, and as most of us lived close to the school, we were allowed to go home. After the 'All Clear' was sounded very few pupils returned to their classes!

Our head master retired on 31st July, the end of the school

year. We then had four weeks holiday. When we returned, I found myself in Class 8, the 'Scholarship Class' with our new teacher, Mr Dutton, or 'Daddy Dutton' as we called him. In this class we were expected to do a lot of hard work. 'Daddy' Dutton was a very good teacher, who had the ability to know who was messing about behind his back when he was writing on the blackboard! Suddenly, a piece of chalk would fly through the air and crash on the head of the startled offender.

The joint ration of butter and margarine, 6oz, could be taken as all butter or all margarine from 22nd July, and as this amount was so small, two weeks ration could be bought at a time.

Mr Charles Hecht Hon Secretary of the Food Education Society said 'Tea should only be taken twice daily, and never late in the evening. It should be warm, not hot, and never given to children'. The tea ration was 2oz per week each.

Our first experience of a night Air Raid came on Saturday 17th August. The siren sounded at thirty eight minutes past midnight. Twelve high explosive bombs were dropped on the dock area, damaging a railway station, grain silo and water mains. A ship was also overturned.

We spent the time of the raid in our Anderson shelter, well wrapped to in blankets and eiderdowns from our beds. The 'All Clear' sounded at 02.29, and after a warm drink, we all went to bed. The following night the same thing happened again only a little later into the night. The warning sounded at 02.18. This time the bombs were a little closer to home. Incendiary bombs were dropped on Eaton Road, a Nursing home, and some houses, caus-ing little damage. The 'All Clear' sounded at 02.59. We had spent the time of the raid in the shelter, and after a warm drink, went to bed.

There was a short break in the night raids until Wednesday 28th when the siren sounded at 23.50. Many high explosive and incendiary bombs were dropped, particularly in the Mossley Hill and Aigburth areas. Mossley Hill Parish Church was severely damaged, together with houses and garages in that area. The raid

19

was over at 04.20, and we made our weary way to bed.

The next night they were back again. This time at 22.22, high explosive and incendiary bombs were dropped in many places except the city centre. This night brought the war very close to home, with incendiary bombs falling on the Dovecot estate, and an oil bomb falling in the back garden of a house in Lordens Road, some two hundred yards from our house. This bomb did not explode, but made a large crater in the garden, and destroyed a shed and blew the curtains off the windows of the house. We went over to see the hole after the bomb disposal squad had been the next day.

Our first casualties occurred this night, with a girl from the senior school, and a boy recently left the school being killed whilst in the shelters in their respective gardens. The 'All Clear' was sounded at 02.50, and we made our way wearily to bed.

We were not getting much sleep these nights and it was difficult for both parents and children to be fully awake during the day following these raids, but the following night they were back again!

At 22.31 on the night of the 30th, the siren sounded and we made our way to the shelter again. This time it was the Everton district, and Mill Road Hospital that was attacked together with the docks and the Mossley Hill area again. Damage was slight this night, and at 02.48 we returned to our beds.

The Board of Education decided that as so many children were arriving late for school after overnight raids, schools would be allowed to start at 9.30 a.m. The night of 31st August-1st September was marked by two raids. The first at 20.48 until 21.41 and again at 00.22 until 03.10.

This time serious damage was done, with the Custom House being set on fire. A shelter in Cleveland Street received a direct hit, and warehouses being set on fire, and their contents destroyed. There was also damage to houses.

On Monday, 2nd September, whilst we were at school, the siren sounded, and obeying the 'Five Minute' rule, we set off for home. We didn't hurry, but played marbles in Stonefield Road, with four other boys. When we turned into Shellingford Road, we heard the sound of an aeroplane flying low over the houses. Looking up we saw it was a German bomber, then we heard what we thought was the sound of hailstones. It was in fact the sound of machine gun bullets hitting the road around us!. We soon ran to the safety of our homes.

This shooting incident is recorded in the senior school log. 'The siren sounded at 12.55 and the all clear at 13.15.

But the sound of firing was heard at 13.50.

We continued to have night raids on the 3rd and 4th, when houses were demolished in the Kensington area. Lark Lane and Ullet Road, Aigburth Vale High School was damaged and the Rope Works in Lodge Lane was badly damaged by fire.

Uncle George had an allotment in Sefton Park. After this raid, he went over to the park to see if there was any damage to the allotment sheds and greenhouses. He found that many of the sheds were scattered all over the area and the greenhouses had all the glass panels shattered. He also found that most of his cabbages, potatoes and onions were high up in the trees, having been blown there by the explosions.

Specific targets were chosen for the raid in the 5th. when Edge Hill Goods Station, and Lister Drive Power Station were attacked. Houses nearby were damaged. Dunlop Rubber works and the Tunnel Road Cinema were also damaged. The next night, Claudia Street Walton, Washington Street and St James Road were badly damaged. The windows of the Anglican Cathedral were also damaged.

Cousin Betty's mother had a cousin, George Sidall, who was Chief Electrician at the Cathedral. He, with his wife, Millie, and their daughter Christine, lived in a house close to the Cathedral in St James Road. It was their nightly plan to go to the Crypt of the Cathedral when the siren sounded, but on this night, he decided that they would stay at home. Unfortunately, their house was hit, and they were all killed. The funeral service was held in the

Grandmother Jane Spratt, Died October 1940.

Cathedral on Wednesday 11th September, conducted by the Lord Bishop. they were interred at Holy Trinity Church, Wavertree.

The raids continued on the 6th and 7th with enemy bombers over the City for five hours, inflicting damage to many businesses and houses. The Cathedral windows and stone work were also damaged again. We had a night of peace and quiet, then they were back again on the night of the 10th for a total of three hours. West Derby and Woolton were badly damaged. We were content to sleep in the shelter, as the nights were not too cold. Our school work was being interrupted, as we were not fully awake after spending so much time in the shelter. Teachers and pupils coped quite well with the situation, which was to get worse, for again, the bombers returned on 12th, 13th, 14th, 15th, 16th and 17th September, when we had a daylight raid at 15.06 in the afternoon. Bombs were dropped near Rootes factory, Speke, damaging houses nearby. This raid lasted thirty six minutes.

At 19.48 that same night they returned again, causing severe damage to houses and shops in the Lockerby Road area. The raid was over by 23.51.

On 17th September the Senior school was inspected for possible use as an emergency Hospital as it was supposed to be in a safe area.

A very heavy raid came on the night of the 18th, when severe damage was caused in many parts of Liverpool. Walton Prison was hit, and a story going round at that time was that a prisoner had escaped with the 'help' of the rescue services. This was finally cleared up many years later, when building work at the prison unearthed the skeleton, later identified as that of the 'escaped' prisoner.

Raids continued on the nights of 21st and 22nd when T.J. Hughes store in London Road was badly damaged. The underground railway was penetrated, and trains badly damaged. the Docks were also attacked with damage to warehouses and a timber yard at Bootle.

On 22nd September the liner *"City of Benares"* was torpedoed and sunk in the Atlantic Ocean, with the loss of 306 children's lives. Only 46 survivors were picked up.

Vernon and I were to have sailed on the next evacuee ship to America. We were to go to dad's sister Edith, who, with her husband Bill, had emigrated to America in 1927. They lived in Buffalo, New York State. They had agreed to take us for the duration of the war, but when news broke of the sinking of the ship, and the loss of life, dad decided that we would stay at home for the rest of the war.

Two separate raids took place on the night of the 23rd, when damage was caused mainly to the North of the City. In the early hours of the 25th the City Centre area of Parker Street, and Clayton Square were severely damaged, together with Silcocks Cattle Food Warehouse, and other establishments on the Dock Road. An early evening raid at 19.25 on the 26th caused extensive damage to Wapping, Kings, Queens, Coburg and Brunswick Docks. Damage was also caused to the Dock Board and Cunard Buildings.

The night of the 27th saw houses demolished in Great Homer Street, and the Council school in Banks Road, Garston damaged. The following night, Everton and Aigburth districts were attacked together with warehouses at the Duke's Dock area.

On the 1st of October, the raid lasted a total of nine minutes. Incendiary bombs were dropped on East Toxteth Dock. There was a lull of a week, before the raids resumed on Monday the 7th, when high explosive bombs were dropped on Stanley Road, Great Mersey Street, Lichfield Road, Wavertree and Grantley Road.

At this time, my grandmother was seriously ill, and grandfather had her bed brought downstairs into the living room of their house in Moss Grove. Vernon and I were taken to see he shortly before she died.

We went with mum and dad to the house on the day of the funeral, and met our cousin Betty. As the Coffin was taken out of the house, all the houses in the street drew their curtains, as a sign of respect. The Coffin was then placed in a glass sided Hearse,

24

which was drawn by four jet black horses, and proceeded to St Bede's Church in Hartington Road for the Funeral Service, and then to Smithdown Road Cemetery for the Burial.

We were considered too young to go to the service or the burial, but stayed at the house with a neighbour, who was preparing the meal for the family's return. As the proceedings were going slowly, it was decided that I should stay at Betty's house, so with uncle George and aunt Alice, I set off for Cairns Street.

We had been there a short while, when the siren sounded at 18.33, and we were taken to a brick-built shelter in the entry at the rear of the house. A few minutes after we had settled down, a woman shouted "It's hail-stoning". Then an Air Raid Warden ran in shouting "It's not hailstones, they're machine gunning us outside".

That night the damage was done to Everton Valley, Knotty Ash, Mossley Hill and Mill Street.

After the raid we went back to the house, where Betty and I were put to bed in a Morrison Shelter in the living room. This shelter was named after Herbert Morrison, a member of the Government, and consisted of a solid table-like construction, with heavy gauge wire net sides. These shelters were given to householders without gardens. We did not sleep for very long, as the siren sounded at 21.36 when further attacks were made on property in Manningham Road and Hogarth Road. The raid was over at 23.22, and we were able to sleep as best we could until the morning. After breakfast, I was taken back to Moss Grove where I was reunited with mum, dad and Vernon.

Betty and her friends, including Alex Hall (whom she was later to marry) would play along Princess Road and would go along Upper Hampton Street where there was a long, low building that had sliding doors onto the street. On several occasions, when the doors were open, they could see Barrage Balloons being made on long benches. The children were not encouraged to loiter around the doors for long, being chased by the workers.

The following night it was the turn of the City Centre to bear the brunt of the bombs during the first raid which started at 18.37, and finished at 19.49. Heavy damage was caused in South John Street, James Street, Redcross Street, Paradise Street, Hanover Street, and South Castle Street. There was also damage in the docks area. The second raid started at 21.00 with the 'All Clear' sounding at 23.23. Damage was caused to Hill Street, and the Bankhall area.

During these raids we had regular visits to Ashover Avenue of a mobile Anti-aircraft Gun. This gun would fire perhaps five or six shells, then drive off to another site.

Dad had to do his share of 'Firewatching' this meant that he would stay the night at his office to watch for incendiary bombs that might cause a fire. This was especially dangerous as he, and other men at the office were watching over tanks holding many thousands of gallons of Oil and Petrol.

It was after one of his turns that he came home after work only to be caught in one of the early evening raids. He managed to travel by the 60 bus to Old Swan, but had to walk the rest of the way. When he arrived at our front door, he couldn't get in, as we were in the shelter. Mum had locked the front door, as there were some people who made a habit of breaking into houses whilst the occupiers were sheltering elsewhere. I should explain that our house was the middle one of three. The houses on either side of us had a side entrance to their back gardens, but ours was round the corner in Shellingford Road. There was a ten foot high brick wall into which our back gate was built, but again mum had bolt-ed the gate as well. Dad went round to try to get in at this gate, but finding it locked, decided to try to climb over the wall. He managed to get to the top of the wall, and was ready to drop down into our garden, when a hand grabbed him, and he was pulled to the ground by a Policeman who had been watching him from across the road. Suspecting him to be a burglar, it took a lot of persuasion on dad's part to convince him that he really did live there.

The following night the bombers were late. The siren sounded at 22.14. Bombs were again dropped on the docks and on Myrtle Gardens, killing eleven, and injuring nine. Severe damage was done to houses in Gadsby Street.

It was on the 13th October that Princess Elizabeth, now 14 years old, made her first radio broadcast to all child evacuees.

Whilst these raids were being carried out on Liverpool, the R.A.F. was taking the bombing to the German people. A raid on Berlin lasted for four hours and heavy damage was reported. Hamburg had a taste of the same treatment.

Italy invaded Greece without warning, and Hitler met with General Franco and Marshall Petain in a Cross-Europe trip by railway.

The radio was a great source of information and entertainment. Cinema Organs were widely used at the start of the war, with Sandy McPherson, Reginald Foort and Reginald Dixon, playing regularly. Early morning programmes included the 'Daily Dozen' a keep fit spot at 7.15 a.m., followed by 'Lift up Your Hearts', and followed after the 8 a.m News, by Dr Charles Hill 'The Radio Doctor'. Other daily programmes were 'Housewives Choice' and 'Workers Playtime'. In the evenings would be `Monday Night at Eight' which included Puzzle Corner, Inspector Hornleigh Investigates, and the East Ender Syd Walker, the Cockney Rag and Bone man, with his views of life in the East End of London. He always ended with "What would you do chums"?

Thursday night would not be complete without I.T.M.A. Tommy Handley with his gang in fun and mayhem, with such characters as Frisby Dyke, played by Derek Guyler, Mrs Mopp, the cleaner (Dorothy Summers), Fumf, (Jack Train), Sam Scram (Sydney Keith), Signor So So (Dino Galvani), Miss Hotchkiss, his secretary, (Diana Morrison), Ali Oop (Horace Percival), and Colonel Chinstrap (Jack Train). Catchphrases from the show became universally used, such as "Can I do yer now, sir?", "I brought this for you, sir", and "I don't mind if I do".

Rob Wilton was also very popular with his sketches as Mr

Muddlecombe, J.P., and the harassed Fire Officer. These were our favourite shows, together with 'The Old Town Hall', which had Richard Goulden playing the part of 'Old Ebeneezer' the watchman, who would start a mini drama each week with the words "One night, as I was sitting round my Fire bucket".

Richard Goulden also played the part of Toad in Kenneth Graeme's The 'Wind in the Willows', a book much loved by me.

Charlie Chester had his Army Show, 'Stand Easy' with characters 'Whippet Quick' the Cat Burglar and 'Ray Ling' the Chinese Fence. Sunday night would Have 'Garrison Theatre' with Jack Warner with his 'Little Gel' with stars of the Music Hall.

There was a fifteen minute spot at 8.45 p.m. when all the National Anthems of the countries fighting on our side were played each week as a sign of solidarity against the foe.

The raid in the 16th lasted from 19.24 until 21.10, and incendiary bombs were dropped on the Walton and Everton districts, hitting a surface shelter, causing about 30 casualties. On the 17th at 21.19 the siren sounded again. A wing of Fazackerley Sanatorium was demolished, killing one patient. Bombs were dropped on houses in West Derby, and an unexploded bomb was found in the yard of the Morrison school, Smithdown Road. The 'All Clear' sounded at 22.39.

The following night it was the turn of Norris Green, and the South end of the City, with St Clement's Church being seriously damaged. This raid started at 19.54 and was over at 22.51.

The 19th saw high explosive bombs being dropped on Tuebrook and the South end of the City again. Shops and houses being demolished in the High Park Street area with St. Silas Church being severely damaged.

The Seaman's Orphanage was hit by a high explosive bomb, which failed to go off, but caused serious damage to the building. This raid started at 19.00 and finished at 23.56.

An early morning raid on the 21st, saw high explosive bombs dropping near to Rootes Aircraft factory in Speke, causing slight damage to overhead electric cables. This raid was at 07.28 and lasted until 07 46.

On the night of the 21st, the raid started at 18.58, with incendiary bombs dropping throughout the City. High explosives were dropped on Dacy Road, severely damaging houses.

Two tram cars were seriously damaged in Priory Road. Damage was also caused to service mains in Aigburth Road, disrupting gas and water supplies.

After a night of peace, the bombers returned on the 25th, at 19.33, dropping bombs on houses in the Richmond Park area, causing serious damage to Holy Trinity school, and a slight fire in the Rope Works, in Mill Lane. The raid was over at 22.03.

The following night Netherfield Road, was heavily bombed, with high explosives demolishing houses and shops. Thirty houses and four Public Houses were badly damaged. Sixteen persons were trapped, the majority of whom perished in the resulting fires. One Warden was killed and another seriously injured. This raid started at 19.29 and continued until 00.58

The following night the siren sounded at 18.01. Nothing seemed to have happened until about midnight, when serious damage by fire, was caused to the sheds of North East Queens Dock. The blaze was soon brought under control, but three firemen were killed. Several other bombs were dropped on the Dock estate, causing only slight damage. The raid was over at 02.15.

On the 29th there were three separate raids. The first was at 11.40 and lasted until 13.04. The second was at 18.54 until 19.19. On both occasions there were no incidents reported. The third raid started at 20.07 with damage being caused in Thomas Street, demolishing warehouses and workshops and shattering windows in the Castle Street area. The Telephone Exchange in South John Street was hit causing temporary disruption to service. Incendiary bombs fell in the Bold Street area and on railway sidings at Speke and on the Match Works at Garston. There were small fires but no serious damage reported. This raid was over at 21.37.

Juvenile car theft is not new. In October a thirteen year old boy stole a car valued at £100 (a lot of money) from opposite the

Rialto Cinema Upper Parliament Street and drove it to Warrington. The car was reported missing, and a Police Constable on Patrol in Warrington spotted it, and calling for a Police car, gave chase along Liverpool Road. The boy drove at 60mph, colliding with a lorry and a bus. The chase ended when he was unable to negotiate a bend and crashed through the railings of a farm, coming to rest in a cabbage patch and being detained by the farmer's son.

The raids started again in the 1st of November at 19.52 when the siren sounded. Incendiary bombs were dropped on County Road, Great Howard Street and East Lancashire Road areas causing slight damage and some small fires. The Raid finished at 21.10 but the bombers returned at 23.52 to do the same thing all over again, finally going home at 12 minutes past midnight.

On the 4th, there were three separate raids. The first at 19.54 lasted fifty four minutes, the second at 00.39, lasted forty nine minutes and the third at 03.42 lasted twenty minutes. During the first raid, high explosives were dropped on Townsend Avenue and Wavertree playground, where two houses were seriously damaged, and fifteen slightly damaged. No damage reported in second or third raids. Seventeen German planes had been shot down since the end of August. These had been mainly destroyed over Anglesey by our Night Fighters.

At school, our new head teacher, Mr Whalley, officially took up his duties on 4th November. Also at this time because of the Air Raids, our milk supply became irregular. Some days we would not have a delivery at all.

At home, mum decided that Vernon and I would have to help in the running of the home and the shopping, as a lot of time was spent standing in queues for rations. It was decided that I would help in the house and Vernon would help with the shopping. As our house was of the double fronted design, we had a very long dining room. It was the style to have Linoleum on the floor with a carpet square in the middle. A smaller rug would be in front of the fire. On Saturday morning, it was my job to scrub the

Linoleum, and if there was any available, give it a coating of floor polish.

Vernon would go with mum to stand in one queue, while she stood in another, waiting for deliveries of food and vegetables.

On the 8th there were six alerts but only a few incendiary bombs were dropped on Childwall Valley, with slight damage to North Farm, Wambo Lane. The 12th saw the raid start at 20.05 with oil bombs on Wavetree Road Post Office and high explosives close to Edge Hill Goods Station, with three houses demolished and several slightly damaged. The Balloon Barrage was not flying due to high winds, so the raiders were able to fly at a low altitude over the City. The raid was over at 21.21.

Six nights passed without incident, until on the 18th the siren sounded at 02.52. Incendiary bombs fell on houses in Guest Street and Warehouses in Sefton Street, causing slight damage but no casualties. Several Barrage balloons came down in flames due to atmospheric conditions. The raid was over at 03.56. On the 19th the raid started at 19.43. with a large number of incendiary bombs falling on Aigburth, followed by high explosives. Damage was caused by fire to houses, two schools and a church. Two houses in Wingate Road were demolished. Other damage was caused in the Anfield area to three houses which were demolished and many others damaged in Teulon Street. The raid was over at 22.52.

The 22nd came and the siren sounded at 22.50. High explosive bombs fell on the Great George Street area causing slight damage to houses and business premises. The raiders went home at 23.04.

It was now getting colder at night, so dad decided to turn the area under our stairs into a shelter. We used to keep our coal supply beneath the stairs in a specially constructed compartment. It was cleaned out, the walls whitewashed and four small seats and an electric light were installed. There was a door which opened onto the kitchen, so we were protected from any blast damage that might occur.

On the 28th we had the heaviest raid so far. The siren sounded at 19.23. and bombs and parachute mines were dropped on the Botanic Park and Durning Road, area where a basement shelter was hit. There were 290 people in the shelter at the time. One hundred and sixty six bodies were finally recovered. Damage was also caused to houses in Rose Place and a Cinema in Commercial Road. The Mines were responsible for damage and fires in Spofforth Road Gas works, and a shed containing sugar at Garston docks. Damage was also caused in Holland Street and Ardleigh Road. Allerton, Wavertree and Childwall received incendiary bombs, one coming down the chimney at Megan and Olwen's home in Freshfield Road setting fire to the floor boards, shattering the windows and blowing out the top panel of the back door. Fortunately they were in a shelter at the time.

Two houses in Micklefield Road were destroyed by a Parachute mine. On this night, thirty Parachute mines were dropped, of which eight failed to explode. The raid ended at 03.58.

A short raid the following night, starting at 22.39 and lasting eleven minutes, saw bombs dropped on the Rathbone Road area, causing little damage.

We were then allowed a lull in the bombing, and went about our daily routine as best we could, trying to learn our lessons, and doing our homework in preparation for the Scholarship examination we were to take in March the following year. It was in this month that Neville Chamberlain, who took us into the war, died.

He had been Prime Minister for three years before his resignation. He was aged 71, and had been ill with Cancer for some time.

At the Education Committee Meeting, Councillor Gordon said "Apart from evacuees, there were at present on Elementary rolls, about 100,000 children, 57,000 full time, 30,000 half time, 6,000 home teaching, plus 7,000 five year olds, having no teaching. There were 163,000 places for Elementary teaching but 25,000 had been lost due to closure, requisitioning or war damage".

The raids re-started on Friday 20th December. We went into

our shelter under the stairs and awaited the noise of the aircraft, guns and bombs. The raid started at 18.20 and went on until 03.58 Saturday morning. The Town Hall and Municipal Buildings were hit and set alight, as were the Cunard Offices and the Landing Stage. A Parachute Mine exploded near the Adelphi Hotel causing considerable damage to surrounding property. The North End Docks were also damaged by many high explosive bombs.

Food shortages were beginning to tell, with such things as carrots replacing dried fruit in Christmas cakes and puddings. No more bananas were being imported and oranges from Spain were in short supply. Lord Woolton the Minister of Food, hinted that an extra ration of tea and sugar could be made for the festivities.

We had another raid in the 21st starting at 18.38 and going on until 05.15 Sunday morning. This raid was very severe causing heavy damage in the City Centre with incendiary bombs setting large areas ablaze. Parachute mines fell close to the Royal Infirmary and again the dock area was severely damaged.

Dad had been rushed to the Royal Infirmary with acute appendicitis and was still under the effects of the anaesthetic, when he was transferred by ambulance to the Floral Hall, Southport, for safety.

We all slept as best we could after these raids and later all the local boys would meet and have a search for shrapnel in the gardens and roads in our area. Some pieces were over six inches long, these coming from Anti-aircraft shells that had exploded in the sky and the pieces falling back to earth. A mornings collection would be put on show and `swaps' would be made for different sized pieces. To have an incendiary bomb case was to be 'King' of the collectors. I didn't have one, but I did see a few that had been brought from the city centre by uncles of some of the boys.

Another night raid followed in the usual pattern, starting at 18.38 and continuing until 06.12 the following morning. Serious damage again to the Dock area and to Rootes factory at Speke. The following night the raid started at 19.08, going on until 01.23

and again damage was caused to the docks.

Two young heroes of one of the December raids were Vincent Costello, fourteen and his nephew George Beckett aged seven. Eight people were trapped in their bombed home and these two boys helped in their rescue. George was eventually dug out of the rubble after being trapped for fifty hours.

During each night of Air Raids, it was estimated that five or six babies were born. We were able to celebrate Christmas with the traditional turkey and plum pudding, but presents were not much in evidence.

The popular hit songs for 1940 were: 'A Nightingale Sang in Berkley Square' and 'Whispering Grass' by the Ink Spots.

1941

The May Blitz

The reality of War soon returned, with a raid on Wednesday 1st January. This started at 21.11. A Sack warehouse was demolished, and further damage to the docks was sustained. The raid ended at 01.51

The following night, a single plane dropped incendiary bombs on the Sandforth Road district, and Newsham Park allotments, setting fire to a stable, but causing no other damage. This raid started at 19.14, and ended at 19.47. We were able to have a good nights sleep for a change.

It was during this month I remember having the worst meal of the war. It was a Saturday, and we had been out shopping. There was little fresh meat available, and for dinner this day, we had a tin of tomato soup, which had been diluted with milk to make it go round the four of us. We also had a plate of boiled potatoes.

Experiments were being made with the rations to try to make them go further. One was to place 4oz of margarine in a bowl, cream it with a fork, then place a quarter pint of milk in a saucepan and bring almost to the boil, lift off the gas and allow to cool to room temperature, than adding a pinch of salt, proceed to whip the milk into the margarine with a fork. The result gave an almost butter like taste and consistency and was used for Sunday tea as a treat.

Our clothes were in constant need of repair and dad had a Cobblers last on which he repaired our shoes, cutting the required heels or soles from a large piece of shoe leather. Our socks were darned and mum taught both Vernon and I to do this task. This was usually done Sunday night, before having our bath ready for school the next morning. We were both bathed together to save water and coal to heat the water. Our short respite from the air raids came to an end on Thursday 9th January, when the sirens sounded the warning at 19.37. The docks at the south end of the City were the target together with Dingle Oil Depot. Dad was not on fire watch duty this night. Some houses were demolished in Virgil Street and fires started in the Everton district. A Dutch barn was burnt out at Holt Farm Gateacre. The all clear sounded at 01.18.

Heavy snow fell on the 17th, causing many problems with transport and with deliveries of food to the shops. The schools were short of coke to heat the radiators and we sat in class wearing our mackintoshes and overcoats as the temperature was just above freezing. During the period of bad weather there were no air raids and we were able to have a good night's rest.

Price controls were placed on many foodstuffs including coffee, cocoa, rice, spaghetti, as certain people were buying large quantities for resale at inflated prices.

It was revealed that the average British household lived on less than £5 per week, with average spending on food being £1.14s.10d, rent 10s.10d, clothes 9s.4d, fuel and light 6s.5d. Other miscellaneous items came to £1.5s.7d. The war is now costing Britain £11 million per day.

The raiders returned on Saturday 15th February when we had three raids. The first started at 13.39 and lasted ten minutes when no bombs were dropped. The second raid started at 19.34 with incendiary bombs being dropped in the Aigburth area, and was over at 20.08. The third raid started 23.23 when the North end of the city was hit with incendiary and high explosive bombs causing only slight damage. The raid was over at 02.06. We then had almost a month without further raids.

The weather played an important part in this with heavy snow falling on the 20th. We were being prepared for our examination at school with Mr. Dutton setting mock papers for us to attempt.

Two raids were inflicted on the city during the night of the 12th March with the first raid starting 19.13 with no incidents, and the raid being over at 19.23. The bombers returned at 20.29 causing heavy damage to the City Centre. Over a hundred fires were started at such places as the Main Post Office, Victoria Street, South John Street Telephone Exchange and the Municipal Annexe, Dale Street receiving hits. This raid was over at 03.56. This night was a very clear night, and running battles could be seen in the sky and several enemy aircraft were shot down. In one incident, ARP messenger boys of small stature were lowered into a cavity under a bombed house to rescue two small children.

The following night the attack started at 20.25 but was not heavy on the city, but bombs caused extensive damage to a shed at Alexandra Dock. Two ships sank in the river during the day, after striking mines. The raid on the 14th started at 20.52 when about two hundred incendiary bombs fell on Speke causing damage to houses and a factory. Kirkdale Railway Station was also hit. This raid was over at 02.36.

A lull of three weeks followed these raids and things at school were as normal as the teachers could make them. We sat the Scholarship examination and the papers were taken away for marking. We continued with our gardening, sowing seeds and planting seed potatoes for later in the year.

April saw the War Budget raise Income Tax to a record 50%. In this month the first 'Soap' was broadcast called 'Front Line Family'. This was the Government's way of getting messages to the people about the best way to use food and to save fuel and help the war effort. This programme continued until 1945, when it was replaced by 'The Robinson Family' which continued until 1947.

The night of the 7th saw explosive incendiary bombs fall on the Beaconsfield Road area, Garston and district and Menlove Avenue. A large number also fell in the Lister Drive area, some on the Power Station. Damage was only slight. Later high explosives fell in the Edge Lane area demolishing a church and damaging a convent. This raid started at 21.35 and was over at 03.45.

A week went by before we were attacked again, when the Garston and Aigburth districts were showered with incendiary bombs. Houses were damaged and eight people were killed in Saunby Street. High explosives were dropped on the Great Homer Street area, causing heavy damage to houses. This raid started at 23.00 and finished at 04.03.

On the 26th the raid started at 22.27 when many parachute mines were dropped between Townsend and Muirhead Avenues. Incendiary bombs fell on other areas of the city causing slight damage. Parachute mines also fell in Ballantyne Road, causing extensive damage and many casualties. There were several unexploded bombs in Ballantyne Road. This raid was over at 01.59

Cousins John and Philip had changed the place they had been evacuated to. From Tattonhall, they were now in North Wales, at a little village called Cwm-y-glo, between Caernarfon and Llanberis. The day before the raid on Townsend Avenue, their mother decided to bring them home for a short visit to the rest of her family, who lived in the area most badly damaged. They were very quickly taken back to the safety of the little Welsh village.

What was to be known as 'The May Blitz' began on Thursday 1st May at 22.34 when the bombers arrived to cause serious damage to a cooked meats factory in New Bird Street, a timber yard in Kempston Street, shops in London Road, and the glass roof of Lime Street Station, houses in the Low Hill district, Grafton Street, West Brunswick Dock, and Cazneau Street. Houses in Claremont, Garmoyle, and Wellington Roads were demolished, together with a very serious fire at Crawfords Biscuits Works in Binns Road. This raid was over by 00.28

The following morning, attendance at school was very low due to the previous nights raid. The following night, Friday the 2nd, the raid started at 22.20. It was a particularly heavy one, with many areas of the city being hit. Serious fire damage was caused to the City Centre, and to warehouses and their contents in

Bridgewater, Norfolk, and Chaloner Streets. Sheds in the Queens Dock area, together with the Dock Board offices, Corn Exchange, a rice mill in Upper Pownall Street, and the Gas Works in Duke Street. A parachute mine dropping in South Castle Street, caused serious damage to shops, two trams cars, and an electricity sub station. The Dock Road was completely blocked, where the overhead railway collapsed. High explosive bombs fell in Lumber Street, causing extensive damage to Exchange Station, shops and offices in the area. A parachute mine fell in Cornwallis Street, seriously damaging several houses.

Large fires and heavy damage was caused in Strand Street and James Street by high explosives. Blast damage was caused to India Buildings, the Cunard Building and the Tunnel building. Dwelling houses in Upper Duke Street, Bedford Street and Pembroke Place were subject to heavy damage. Parachute mines caused heavy damage to houses in Linnet Lane, Ullet, Waverley, Mannering, Coltart and Kingsley Roads.

It was in this area the Betty lived. She had been a pupil at St. Margaret's Higher Grade School, but like so many of us, she had had very little schooling. Her school had been bombed early in 1940. She had a teacher. Miss Thompson, who came to her house, and to her friend Audrey Price's house in Solway Street, twice a week. Several other girls from the area came as well for two hours tuition, twice a week. When she sat the Scholarship examination at Blackburne House, she like me failed. She didn't know what a fraction was!

After the home lessons, she was sent to St. James' School, opposite the Anglican Cathedral. It was great fun at this school, as the playground was on the roof. When the siren sounded at playtime, the children would run down to the basement to shelter.

At home, at the beginning of a raid her dad would close wooden shutters over their windows, and they would sit at the top of the cellar stairs, where they thought they would be safe. On the night that the mines fell in Coltart Road, they were sitting at the top of the cellar steps. There was a vivid flash of light through the coal grid set in the front step, and a terrific explosion. All the plaster fell off the walls, and the place was filled with choking dust. The whole house shook to its foundations, and the sound of breaking glass was everywhere.

When the raid was over, they came out from the cellar, and her dad lit a candle. Betty burst out laughing, as her dad had about two inches of soot stuck to his hair, and they were all covered in plaster and dust. The wooden shutters and been blown off the wall and were on the dining table. All the glass had gone from the windows and was lying on the furniture and floor.

Other areas of the city to be damaged that night included Wapping Overhead railway station, Grafton and Buckland Streets, St. Brigid's church and crypt air raid shelter, which was partially demolished. High explosives fell on St. Athanasius Church, Fountains Road, and houses in Chancel Street. Parachute mines fell on Hunslet and Donsby Roads, the Railway Signal works, and Adlam Crescent.

Other parachute mines fell in Bowland Avenue close to my uncle George and aunt Laura's home. Maple Grove, Egerton Road, The Ministry of Pensions Hospital, Park Avenue, Ibbotsons Lane and Smithdown Road cemetery, all causing extensive damage.

Aunt Gwladys and cousin Harold still lived in Salisbury Road with Aunt Mabel. When the siren sounded they would push the table out of the dining room and wedge it under the stairs as a shelter. It was this night that the explosions close by caused by a parachute mine, blew in the front windows of the house. At the end of the raid, Aunt Mabel called out "Gwladys, come into my room as yours has gone". She meant that all the window glass had been blown out. Repairs with the wartime frosted glass were carried out as quickly as possible.

High explosives fell in Ullet, Glenconner, Childwall Valley and Childwall Abbey Roads, and Fern Grove, all causing serious damage. A parachute mine fell on Pemberton Road causing extensive damage to houses and Old Swan Police Station suffered blast damage. Oil incendiary bombs fell on the Automatic Telephone Company factory in Binns Road causing fires. The raid was finally over at 02.37. If we thought the last nights raid was bad, we had not reckoned on what was to come on the following night, the 4th.

This was to be the night when the Luftwaffe dropped 66,000 incendiary bombs on the city. It started at 22.30 and gas, water and electricity mains were to be seriously damaged. The Central Telephone Exchange was completely cut off.

Lewis's and Blacker's stores were gutted by fire and the area bounded by Lord Street, Paradise Street and Canning Place was devastated. Wolstenholme Square, Leyton Paper Mills, Henry Street, the Tatler Cinema Church Street, Salvage Corps Headquarters Hatton Garden, Head Post Office Victoria Street, Littlewoods Building Church Street, Government Buildings Crosshall Street, Museum and Library William Brown Street, Magistrates Court, Customs House, Central Railway Station and India Buildings were all seriously damaged. Large fires caused damage to Princes, Dukes, Canning and Salthouse Docks, East Wapping Basin, Warehouse in Gower Street and Riverside Station. A parachute mine fell on Mill Road Infirmary causing many casualties and very heavy damage. Seventeen houses were demolished in Alt Street.

It was the following morning that Betty and her friends went to the top of Cairns Street on the corner with Kingsley Road and stood watching rescue parties digging out people from the ruins of their homes. Their faces blank with incomprehension. She remembers seeing a friend being dug out, dead. She was wearing a blue velvet dressing gown, and her arm hung down limp over the side of the stretcher. She has always to this day wanted a blue velvet dress. The following day, playing with friends, she found a piece of thick plaitted rope in the yard of the house at the back of hers. It was grey outside with white strands inside. They used it for a skipping rope until someone told them it was off the parachute mine that had fallen on Alt Street.

41

For the rest of the air raids she and her parents used a communal shelter built into the yard of a neighbours house. This shelter was for about five families to share. As she always had cats, she would take her cat to the shelter in her school hat (one of the navy blue pudding basins with a wide brim).

One night she became separated from her mum and dad. All hell had let loose with searchlights, guns flares and bombs dropping. She was eventually found by a warden in hysterics running up and down the entry clutching her hat complete with cat. She was reunited with her parents, but to this day she is terrified of thunder and lightning. She has to go into a cupboard or somewhere completely enclosed so that she cannot see the flashes.

Shelters were damaged in Gildarts Gardens, Addison Street schools, Anthony and Vulcan Streets. Parachute mines fell in Stanley, Carisbrook and Fountains Roads, Newman, Freeland and Index Streets, Margaret and Peter Roads and Dallas Grove, causing severe damage and many casualties. Two wings of Walton prison were demolished and Kirkdale Railway Station was hit.

High explosives caused heavy damage to houses and shops in Kirkdale and Walton areas. Fires caused serious damage to Kinross Mill, Tillotsons Paper and Printing Works. Walton Parish Church was destroyed and Walton Police Station slightly damaged. More docks were damaged by parachute mines and high explosives. One ship SS *Malakand* loaded with ammunition caught fire and exploded at 09.00 hours on the 4th of May, causing widespread damage in which several barges and a coaster were sunk. Sudley Road and Rose Lane Council schools were seriously damaged as was the Corporation Yard in Smithdown Road. Breckside Corporation Depot and an underground shelter at the junction of Queens drive and Edge Lane Drive were hit. An ammunition train caught fire at Breck Road siding with resultant damage to houses over a wide area. Anfield and Leyfield Road schools suffered extensive damage.

At 04.50 the raiders turned for home and we were so tired we could hardly sleep. There was very little rest on the Sunday, as

Workers in the Littlewoods Parachute Factory, Hanover Street, which was destroyed during the May Blitz.

many people turned into work or to help in the clearing up operations in the city centre. Dad went to the Dingle oil Installation to see what damage had been done. When he came home he brought news of the terrible destruction that had been caused.

They came again on the 5th at 23.58, dropping high explosives on the Belgian Seamen's Hostel, great George Street. Houses were demolished in Catherine, Fairy, Mountjoy and Magnum Streets. Serious damage was caused to the Clinic in Northumberland Street. St. Sylvester's school and the Rotunda Theatre were destroyed by fire. The Gas Works in Athol Street had a direct hit, demolishing one gas holder. Hadfields Fertiliser Works were badly damaged. Walton Lane School was badly damaged by a parachute mine and four houses were demolished in Bingley Road. This raid continued until 04.26.

On Monday morning the 5th of May, owing to the severe raids over the weekend, many boys were absent from school. Miss Mann and Mr Dutton were also absent. Some boys had gone with their parents to try to find members of their families in other parts of the city. Mum and dad's friends, the Court family, had gone to try to find Mrs Court's mother. They had a dog called Peter and we were asked to look after him whilst they were away. He was good and caused no trouble. Vernon and I were very sorry to see him go home.

On the 6th, they were five minutes late arriving! The warning sounded at 00.03. Serious damage was caused by high explosives to St. Nicolas Church Pier Head. Lancelot's Hey, the Salvation Army Hostel Park Lane, South Castle Street, Dukes Grain warehouse, West Kings Quay and South Canning Dock. The Chemical Works in Hardy Street and Park Lane, Great George Street Congregational Church, St Luke's Church and surrounding property. Also, the Gas Offices in Duke Street. Ward 2 of the Royal Infirmary and the Nurses Home Mulberry Street. T. J. Hughes London Road, tenements in Northumberland Street, houses in the the Lodge Lane area. A public house in Christian Street was demolished and the Emido Flour Mills Glasgow Street seriously

44

damaged. Serious damage was also caused to houses in Harvey Street and Smithdown Road.

Salt water mains were used to a great extent to control the fires in the centre of the city. The whole area around Bold Street and Colquitt Street was very badly affected by fire.

On the 7th, the raiders returned at 00.20. Heavy damage throughout the city was caused by both incendiary and high explosive bombs and fires were extensive. The more serious being in the Renshaw Street, Duke Street area. Salt water was used on many of these fires. There was a small fire at the Anglican Cathedral.

My grandfather and three aunts lived in Moss Grove, off Lodge Lane, but during these raids they came to stay with us as it was considered a safer area. Each night they would come, two aunts straight from their offices in town and Aunt Mary who was the 'Housekeeper' to her sisters and father would arrive in time for dinner. The following morning Aunts Florence and Leah would go straight to work and Mary and granddad would return home. It was a very busy household with five people trying to use the bathroom and get ready for work and school. At night we would all settle down to sleep downstairs, all that is, except granddad who was deaf and insisted on going upstairs to bed. "Hitler will not upset my sleeping habits" he said.

It was after this raid, on returning home they found all their windows blown out. The emergency repair team were soon on the spot, boarding up the window space until wartime glass could be fitted. They were among the many who travelled out of the city each evening, finding shelter wherever they could. Sometimes with relatives or friends or just in the country lanes and fields to be out of the danger that fell out of the sky.

One night they returned to our house with a tale about Batty's Dairy in Arundel Avenue, where they used to buy their milk. Mr Batty and his son together with nineteen cows were buried under the debris of their building when it was hit by a bomb. One cow was blown out of the building into the road. A policeman was

45

supposed to have crashed into it on his bicycle in the blackout.

Back at school both Miss Mann and Mr Dutton were still absent and a Miss Jarman arrived to take Miss Mann's class. The following night the 7th the raid started at 23.53 with high explosive bombs falling on the Parcels Office in Hatton Garden, slight damage was caused to the Town Hall. The Landing stage and ferry goods stage also received hits. A serious fire broke out in the Custom House and Bent's Brewery, Johnson Street. St Catherine's Church Abercromby Square was destroyed by fire. Incendiary bombs fell on Mill Street Police Station. Serious damage caused to Wilson's Flour Mills, Mill Street, East and West Harrington sheds and South Coburg shed. The service pipe at Dingle Oil jetty was damaged. High explosives fell on Brunswick Gardens tenements causing serious damage and also on Cheshire Lines Railway damaging the permanent way. Ships in Bramley Moore Dock were damaged and two barges sank in South Stanley Dock. An engineering works in Charters Street was gutted by fire. There was also damage caused by faulty AA shells exploding on houses. This raid was over by 04.07.

What was to be the last night of the May Blitz started by the sounding of the siren at 00.02. This night was to see heavy damage throughout the city caused by high explosive, incendiary bombs and oil incendiary bombs, Tower Buildings, Water Street, and Morris & Jones warehouse, Sir Thomas Street were hit, causing serious damage. A tram car was damaged at the Pier Head, a workshop in Pembroke Place and a builders yard in Fairclough Lane were gutted by fire.

Serious fires broke out at the Cooperage, Gildarts gardens and Stables, Dickson Street. Surface air raid shelters demolished in Beatrice Street and Norris Street. Many houses in the Scotland Road area were demolished. A parachute mine fell in Sandholme Street and Teulon Street destroying houses and three air raid shelters. Many churches and schools were destroyed. Rolling stock at Bankhall carriage sidings was destroyed. Stanley Road Bridge over the railway was smashed. A warehouse in Townsend Street demolished. Serious damage to Sandon Motor Works, Grundy Street, A.F.S. Station, Forth Street, Lambeth Road School, Distillery, Juniper Street, a shelter in Townsend Street, B & A Tobacco Factory, Commercial Road, Carnarvon Road and Rice Lane received many hits, as did Walton Hospital.

Serious damage to North Docks, sheds and railway sheds. Three ships were sunk. A parachute mine fell on Daffodil Road causing damage to houses. The raiders finally left at 04.25.

So ended a very serious attempt to destroy the City of Liverpool and its people. An attempt that failed miserably.

On Friday 8th May, the head teacher was called home to attend to aid raid damage to his home.

We returned to school on the 11th to find our teacher was still absent. There was a story that had been blown up when the ammunition train had exploded on the night of the 3rd of May. Much later it emerged that he had been on duty as an Air Raid Warden when the train exploded. The damage caused to property close to the railway sidings had demolished his house and he had been trying to find accommodation for himself and his family before returning to school.

He returned to school the next day.

On the 15th all our gas masks were examined and where necessary replaced. On the 16th the head teacher had a meeting with Mr Hanson of Hansons Dairies Ltd. Regarding the future supply of milk. No glass bottles were available and no deliveries had been made to the school in the last ten days. It was agreed that future supplies would be in bulk containers.

We had twenty one days without hearing the siren but at 00.51 on the 29th we had another visit from the Luftwaffe. High explosive bombs were dropped in fields growing wheat on Croxteth estate and an army unit nearby. Eight houses in the Beaumont Street area sustained damage, the raid was over at 03.53. They returned at 01.00 on the 31st to drop incendiary bombs on North Corburg, N.W. Toxteth, N.E. Brunswick Docks and Coburg Grain warehouse. High explosive bombs were dropped on StanleyPark

47

Avenue damaging an electricity main and a water pipe in Pinehurst Avenue. Two previously damaged houses were also demolished, the raid was over by 03.30.

The following night, 1st June, saw raiders arrive at 00.37. They dropped incendiary bombs on the Gladstone Dock area causing very little damage. High explosives also fell in this area causing damage to masonary at the North Gladstone shed and Alexandra Dock Quay and Hornby shed by fire. High explosives fell in County Road and Breeze Hill causing damage to three houses.

Clothes rationing was introduced on the 2nd and we had to use margarine coupons for a short time. We all had a total of 66 coupons to last for a year. To clothe us boys in one complete out-fit for school took thirty five coupons. We had to be very careful how we played at, and after school. I imagine secondhand clothes shops did a very good trade. Younger brothers and sisters usually got hand-me-downs.

Our gas masks were again examined on the 9th by the local wardens who were checking on the repairs and replacements required from last months inspection.

We had twenty four days without a raid, then on 25th the siren sounded at 01.12, two high explosive bombs fell on a hut on a nursery in Macketts Lane and another on the loco sheds at NE Princes Dock causing considerable damage. Incendiaries in the Rose Hill area caused fires in a church and a disused house. An AA shell caused damage to aircraft at Linner Road, Speke. The raid was over at 03.35. There were no raids until the night of the 24th when at 01.27 the sirens sounded again. High explosive bombs fell on a hut on a nursery in Macketts Lane and another on the loco sheds at NE Princes Dock causing considerable damage. Bombs also fell on West Waterloo Dock and incendiaries fell in the Rose Hill area, setting fire to a church and an empty house.

On the 27th the announcement of Passes to the City's High Schools was made, but my name was not among the successful.

Coal rationing was introduced on 4th July with each household being allowed forty bags per year.

Grandfather, John Vernon Spratt, died February 1942. (Circa 1905).

Mr Spargo, P.A.C. Superintendent called at the school on the 21st, under the authority of the Director of Education, to inspect the premises and its facilities for use as a rest centre in an extreme emergency, just before we broke up for the summer holiday of four weeks. Before the new school year commenced, Mr Dutton was called up for active service.

An air raid took place on Thursday the 24th at 01.27. The only damage reported was caused by anti-aircraft shells falling on houses in the North end of the city, in County Road and Everton districts. These shells failed to explode in the air, but doing so on hitting houses. This raid was over at 03.17.

When I started at Grant Road, the senior school, nobody told us at the junior school where to go or to whom to report, when we broke up for the summer holiday. It was very strange going into the playground for the first time. After assembly, we were taken back into the hall and a roll call was made. We were then told which class we would be going into and introduced to our teachers. I was in class 1A, with Mrs Leather, an older lady teacher.

We were taught English, Maths, Geography, History, Woodwork, Chemistry, Physics, Music, Art and Technical Drawing.

Mr Elliott was the woodwork master. At the start and end of each of his lessons the tool cabinets of each work bench would be inspected and each tool had to be accounted for.

Our first lesson in woodwork consisted of becoming used to the various types of saw, chisel and plane, and to be familiar with their uses. As we progressed we were shown how to make various joints and when we could do a simple tongue and groove joint, we were given what is now called a 'project'. This was to draw a plan for a cigarette box. Then we had to choose the wood and start to make it. When finished, we were introduced to the mystery of veneering and French polishing.

This project took us many months to perform as we only had one hour per week in this class. Mr Price took us for Chemistry and Music. Many a fine smell came from the Chemistry Lab.

when we were let loose!

There was a 'House' system in the school. There were four 'houses' Childwall, Huyton, Knowsley and Roby, these were denoted by the colours, red, green, blue and yellow. I was placed in Roby House. Our House Master was Mr Price, and once a month for the last hour on Friday afternoon there would be house meetings. At these meetings the Master would encourage the members to strive for greater glory of the House. Teams would be chosen to play the other Houses at football, cricket, and athletics, as each sports season came around.

There was also a system of Stars and Stripes awarded for good behaviour and work or bad behavior and work. A board was placed on the wall in the Quadrangle with the names and houses of boys who had been given stripes for bad behaviour or work. If your name appeared on this board three or more times in one week you were awarded detention and if your name appeared more than twelve times in a month you would be sent to the Head Teacher for more serious punishment - usually the cane. The Star chart would be added up for good behaviour and the House with the most stars in a month won a shield.

We were given homework from the start, usually a different subject each night with extra for the weekend.

School started at 9am until 12 O'clock, and 1.30 p.m to 4 o'clock.

Our next air raid was on Wednesday 22nd October, at 20.51. There were no bombs dropped, but damage was again caused by Anti-aircraft shells falling on houses in the city. The `All Clear' sounded at 23.57. The last raid of this eventful year took place on Saturday, 1st November at 21.07, when high explosive bombs were dropped on a cottage in a wood on the Croxteth Estate. Slight damage was caused. An AA Nose Cap fell on a house in Lomond Road causing slight damage. This raid was over at 23.02.

The 7th of December saw the Japanese attack on the U.S. Fleet at Pearl Harbour, sinking or seriously damaging five battleships, fourteen other ships and destroying two hundred aircraft.

They also killed 2,400 people.

Now we were looking forward to the Christmas holiday and to going to the Pantomime at the Pavilion Theatre. This time it was 'Cinderella' with Albert Burdon. Other supporting performers were Bartlett and Ross, Mavis Whyte, Sybil Dunn and Company.

Hits of 1941 were 'Boogie-Woogie Bugle Boy', 'White Cliffs of Dover' and 'Blues in the Night'.

ist

1942

"War" Declared on Finch Hall

We returned to school on Wednesday 7th January after the Christmas and New Year holiday. It was very cold and there was a thick fog. Heating in the school was not very good as there was a shortage of coke to burn in the boiler that heated the water in the radiators.

On Saturday the 8th we had the first air raid of the year. The siren sounded at 22.57 and high explosive bombs were dropped in Stanhope Street and Upper Stanhope Street causing the demolition of houses. This raid was over by 01.15.

At school, we were all examined by the nurse on the 14th. Six boys required treatment for various problems.

A very heavy fall of snow during the night of the 19th caused the roads to be blocked. Only one hundred and seven boys were in school to answer the register.

Alterations to the Craft Room were started on the 28th in preparation for the distribution of meals. A sink, a geyser, which was taken out of the Science Laboratory, a drain board, cupboards and shelves were installed.

We were to have an A.T.C. Squadron based at the school and a Mr. Saunders came to see the head with a view to using certain rooms for three nights per week.

A letter regarding the serving of mid-day meals had been sent out before Christmas and the resulting return of applications for meals revealed that eighty five boys wanted them. The Evening Institute was well into its new term when the Head decided to spend an evening seeing exactly what took place. He was very impressed with all the activities being enjoyed by a large number of boys.

Mr. Clark was a leader in his own profession and he was a regular contributor to the Teachers Journal `Teachers World'. He directed teachers attention to the problem of extraneous duties, which, he wrote, are assuming alarming proportions. He wrote a poem called `Cargoes' with apologies to John Maesfield:-

Petty cash and savings, clothing and gardening.
Pension forms and staffing sheets and probationers reports.
Requisitions, stock books.
Inventory and record cards.
Employment forms and "syllabi" and letters of all sorts.
Dinner tickets, test papers, time book and medicals.
Receipt books, staffing forms, parents notes and clinic cards.
Repairs book, dental cards.
Tram tickets, entrance forms.
Rota for the yard.
Leavers lists, admission book.
Fuel cards and "C.P.'s".
Monthly forms for tenancy.
Blue forms for salaries.
Schemes of instruction for As, Bs and Cs.
Myriad's of circulars from the Education Office.
To read, mark, learn to do or to belay.
Giving information of milk, meals and vacancies.
Fire watching holidays and deductions from pay.

Sport in general was very well supported, and in February, boxing took centre stage with teams being selected to oppose Finch Hall School. Late in the month the Northern Counties Schoolboys Championships were held at Lowe House Boys Club in St. Helens. We topped the lists with four boys being selected for the 5st. title and three for the 6st. title. One boy was selected for the 6st. 7lb title. Over forty contests took place. We also had a chess team and they were playing against Finch Hall school.

My grandfather was buried on Tuesday 10th February. Mum and dad went to the funeral with Vernon and I going to the house in Moss Grove. Betty was there with our youngest cousin Harold, but John and Philip were still evacuated.

We were allowed to play records on Aunt Leah's gramophone. She had a collection of records by Sandy Powell, a well known comedian of the day. There was also a copy of the 'Laughing Policeman'.

Whilst the family were at the cemetery the neighbours came in and prepared the food for the returning mourners. Points coupons would have been collected from members of the family to enable them to buy tinned meat and whatever else was available at the time.

It was about this time that the first American soldiers came to Huyton. Their camp was in Blue Bell Lane and there were about 2,000 men, mostly coloured. There was quite an amount of resentment amongst the local population, especially the men, as the girls flocked to the gates to meet the soldiers.

Monday the 24th saw the opening of the school mid-day meal service with seventy four boys and eighty four girls having a meal. The following day, Councillor S.C. Saltmarsh, Chairman of the Meals Committee called to inspect arrangements.

During March the following activities were taking place on the school premises:-

Emergency Feeding Centre, School Canteen, Evening Institute, Play Centre, Women's Technical Classes. A.T.C. and G.T.C. Special classes for mentally and physically handicapped children. The school was also delegated as a 'Shadow' Hospital.

George Harvey had an accident in the Science Laboratory due to him tipping back on his stool and cutting his head on a radiator. He was given first aid by members of staff and was sent to Alder Hey Hospital, where he was detained.

For my twelfth birthday on 10th April, which was a Friday, Dad managed to obtain a pair of football boots and a real leather ball (all second hand of course!) One boot had the nails coming

55

through but he soon sorted that out. We had a shoe repairers last and a few good and well aimed blows with a hammer soon flattened the offending nails.

Dad would put plates on the toes and heels of our shoes which were bought a size larger so that we could 'grow into them' and when the shoes were new the heels of our socks soon went into holes, so darning was a regular job.

It was about this time that news came of my Uncle Leslie, dads youngest brother, being captured by the Japanese somewhere in the Far East. He was in the Royal Air Force just like dad had been.

The day following my birthday I was taken by dad to Anfield to see Liverpool play Everton in the War Cup Competition.

We went to the match on a football special tram which took us from outside our front door to the ground. There were many trams running from all over the city to the game. They would be put into a parking siding close to the ground ready to the take the spectators home again after the game.

We went in the Kop and dad made sure that there was a metal support at our backs. He explained that the crowd would push forward when the team playing into the Kop end was attacking so that they could get a better view of the action. The teams for that day were:-

Liverpool - Hobson, Gutteridge and Lambert, Taylor, Bushe and Kaye, Nieuwenhuys, better know as 'Nivvy', Carney, Dane, Haydock and Liddell.

Everton - Burnett, Cook and Jackson, Bentham, Keen and Curwen, Owen, Mercer, Jones (T.G.), Stevenson and Anderson. Referee:- Mr. F.W. Wort of Nottingham.

Everton had to make two late changes owing to Lawton and Caskie not turning up. There was end to end play but Everton took command and in the 37th minute scored through Jones. Six minutes into the second half Everton increased their lead through Anderson. Liverpool staged a revival and only heroic work by full back Jackson assisted by Burnett in goal, saved them from conceding a goal. Burnett saving brilliantly three times in four minutes. Ten minutes from the end, Mercer went off injured. Three minutes from time Gutteridge handled the ball in the penalty area, but Hobson in the Liverpool goal saved from Cook's penalty attempt.

The attendance was 30,000, final score Liverpool 0 Everton 2. The second leg was played at Goodison park the following Saturday, Liverpool won 1-0, but Everton progressed to the next round by an aggregate of 2-1.

Vernon and I became more aware of the children living in Ashover Avenue. I remember Bill Jones who lived at no. 17 and Billy Davies at 21. Further along the Avenue lived Harry James at 27 and Walter Bloor at 39. On our side, were the Farrell family who lived next door to us. There was Sheila, Tommy, Warwick and Neal at that time. Norman Burgess lived at 16 and Ken Wilson at 30, Donald Quine at 36. We became aware of girls in the Avenue, with Beryl Day at No. 5 and the Dix sisters, Phyllis, Dorothy and Elsie at 62.

There was also a girl living at No. 20, who went to a private school. (Her father was reputed to be a Bank Manager). He would leave for work each morning immaculately dressed in a suit with white winged collar and Homburg hat, with briefcase, umbrella and newspaper. He would walk to the Crosville bus stop on Liverpool Road.

This was the last stop that Crosville was allowed to pick up passengers coming into Liverpool. The fares were also dearer than Liverpool Corporation trams. She was not allowed to play out with us. I think their name was Tomlinson.

There was the Court family from Stonefield Road, Gladys and Jim, who had four children, Edna, Norman, Joyce and Edwin. Jim was a tram driver and he and his wife Gladys would go to the Conservative Club at Dovecot with mum and dad.

There was also Mr. & Mrs. Luya, who had a son Gordon, with whom we played They also had a daughter Doreen, who was some years older than any of us. Mr. Luya worked for a printer in Liverpool as a Book Binder. They lived in Shellingford Road.

Opposite them was Stan Reid who lived on the corner of Alstonfield Road, Stan's dad was also a tram driver.

As the days were becoming warmer and the daylight hours longer, we would play out with the boys in the avenue. Opposite our house, on East Prescot Road was a field that used to be a haven for gypsy families with their gaily painted caravans and horses.

However, as this field was seen to be a possible landing ground for gliders in any invasion, along with other open spaces throughout the country, it was dug up with trenches and earth mounds to prevent anything landing safely. This was like heaven to us lads.

Soon a 'war' was declared on the boys from Finch Hall. Pitched battles would take place after school with huge lumps of clay and sods flying through the air. At times we were driven out of the trenches and back along Ashover Avenue. We would regroup, find whatever ammunition we could and carry out a 'charge' over Prescot Road and back into the trenches. On more than one occasion a tram driver would stop his tram and chase us as we pelted his vehicle with sods.

In all these battles I don't ever recall anyone being seriously hurt. At the end of the day we would make our way home convinced that we were the winners!

The boys in the Avenue started to join the Boys' Brigade at the Holy Spirit Church, Dovecot. At first only two joined as they were friends of the brother of the young man who was in charge. His name was Ronald Peterson, and he would be about seventeen years old at that time.

I joined on Friday 8th May, 1942, going with Bill Jones, Billy Davies, Harry James, Ken Wilson and Walter Bloor.

Ron Peterson was a Staff Sergeant, the Officers of the Company (the 60th Liverpool) having been called up for Military Service, he together with another boy kept the Company running. We would parade on Friday night in the Church Hall at 8pm. There we would be inspected, and those who had a uniform were expected to have cleaned and polished the buckle of the belt, and

Barrage balloons being assembled at Littlewoods Walton Factory 1942.

made sure the two white lines around the cap were clean, together with the Company numbers.

The uniform consisted of a 'Pill Box' cap of dark blue material with two parallel white lines around the sides and a white button on the top. The company numbers in silver metal were fitted at the front. This cap was worn on the right side of the head, two fingers width above the right eye and was held in place by a chin strap. A white haversack was worn over the right shoulder and secured to the left hip by a brown leather belt which had a brass buckle which was to be polished. A dark blazer or coat was all that was required to complete a very simple but striking uniform, which had been designed many years previously. After inspection there would be short prayers, then a period of Foot Drill. This was to smarten up your attitude and make you obey commands. This would be followed by a period of physical training and at the end of the evening there was a Band Practice. There were about thirty boys who regularly attended both the Friday evening Parade Night and the Sunday morning Bible Class. This was held at 10.30am in the church hall and was taken by the senior boys, it consisted of hymns, prayers and a short talk, and lasted about thirty minutes.

Once a month would be a Church Parade when the Company would parade in uniform and attend the 11am Morning Service. Afterwards, we would march behind the band around the district. I am sure we all felt very proud in our uniform.

On Saturday 25th April, Princess Elizabeth, then sixteen years old, registered for War Service.

The R.A.F. continued its bombing of German cities with the Baltic Port of Lubeck being devastated. This so enraged Hitler that he ordered every British City in the Baideker Guide Book to be razed to the ground.

Advertisements in magazines and newspapers were of a military nature, such as Kolynos Dental Cream showing a W.A.A.F. Officer with pearl white teeth, smiling through the beam of a searchlight. Tubes were priced at 2/2d, 1/3d and 7d including tax.

This was called the 'Economical Tooth Paste'.

Empire Day was celebrated on Friday 22nd May. Parents were invited to school and the programme was taken entirely by the boys and girls.

Hymn	Jerusalem
Prayers	Prayers for Empire
Empire Message	Rt.Hon.Viscount Cranbourne
Song	Motherland O Peaceful England
Song	Canada The Maple Leaf for Ever
Song	Australia Waltzing Matilda
Poem	India The Shawl
Song	S. Africa A Hunting Song
Song	New Zealand The Maori Lament
Speech	Empire
Hymn	O' Beautiful My Country
	National Anthem
	Benediction

The head teacher removed the school captain for unsatisfactory conduct on 25th, and on the 29th he gave a talk to the whole school on smoking. He later investigated several individual cases and suitable action was taken.

The school was finally given a telephone on 3rd July. This was placed in the head's office, and the number was Huyton 1617.

We broke up for the summer holiday on 10th July. On the following day Robert Whiteside was killed, falling off an air raid shelter in Preston, whilst visiting relatives.

During the holidays it was government policy to encourage 'Holidays at Home' due to the restrictions on travel. We were encouraged to travel short distances only to places like New Brighton, Hoylake, West Kirby and Southport. As a family we used to like to go to West Kirby by train from Central Station. We would use the British restaurant in West Kirby where we would enjoy lunch and then go to the beach, having tea again at the restaurant before catching the train back to Liverpool.

Wednesday the 24th saw twenty four boys enter for Royal Life

Saving Certificates, gaining fifteen elementary and nine intermediate certificates. The head teacher praised Mr. Elliott who gave so much of his spare time to train them, and of course, to the boys for their efforts.

The last item to be put on ration during the war was sweets, and this happened on Saturday the 27th, such things as Zubes and Cough Candy, together with Nippets and Victory V lozenges were not on the list of rationed sweets as these were considered to be medicinal. The only other item to be rationed was bread, but this took place in 1946.

Just as we were preparing to return to school on 10th August, on the night of the 9th, the Air Raid sirens sounded at 23.59. Flares were dropped over several districts but no bombs were dropped and the all clear sounded at 01.19. This was to be last raid on the city.

On the 11th Miss Gillies joined the senior school teaching staff from the Junior school.

Salvage collections continued each week and in the last six months twenty eight tons had been collected by the school. We were tenth in the city with an average of two and a half cwt. per boy. The salvage collection included paper, tins, cardboard, string, rags, in fact, anything that could be re-used. The third year boys would go out to the various shopping areas around the school on Monday, Wednesday and Friday morning. One cloakroom was given over to the storage of the collection which was then collected by the Council Refuse Department and taken to a central sorting point.

An exhibition of athletic activities was held on 27th. at Wavertree Playground. Four male teachers went to act as referees.

Thursday 3rd September was a National Day of Prayer, both departments met in the hall to hear a service on the wireless at 11am. This service lasted fifteen minutes.

On Monday 26th October children of both departments were weighed and measured for additional clothing coupons. These were both for boys and girls who were taller or heavier than average. Twenty four girls and fifteen boys qualified for additional coupons. The previous day saw the weekly ration of fresh milk reduced to two and a half pints per person.

At the end of this week class 2A (our class) having obtained 100% in attendance and punctuality for one week were permitted an extra thirty minutes play time.

We were notified at assembly on Friday 30th October, that the school was now 3rd in the city for salvage collection with a total of 59610 lbs.

Thursday 5th November saw an outbreak of sore throats and the head encouraged us to gargle regularly. Dr. Stalybrass, the schools Medical Officer, was applied to for Diphtheria inoculation forms.

The 25th saw the start of making of toys in Handicraft classes, for children in school nurseries.

The following day, 26th, was American Thanksgiving Day, the school assembled to listen to a wireless programme at 2.40pm.

Wednesday 16th December, three boys won bronze medals from the Life Saving Society. Thanks again to Mr. Elliott for his training.

After serving for six months in the 60th Liverpool Company of the Boys' Brigade, Harry James and I decided to transfer to the 1st Roby Company, meeting in St. Andrews Church Hall, Dinas Lane on Tuesday evenings. Everything about this company was so different from the 60th. There was the Captain Rev. C.R. (Dickie) Jarvis, Vicar of Roby who had founded the company in 1936, and his Officers, Messrs. Tom Hunt, Ted Pinnington, Fred Bowler, Tom Rushton and Mr. Barlow. I never got to know his christian name. He was a gentle man who was retired due to having a heart complaint. He was to be my Squad Officer for a number of years. When Harry and I joined we were No. 95 and 96 on the roll. The company was divided into four squads of twenty plus boys. Then each squad had a Lieutenant, Sergeant, Corporal and Lance Corporal. There were also four Staff Sergeants who didn't belong to any squad. They would take turns in parading the

Company at 8pm. before handing over to the Captain for prayers and inspection. Like the 60th, the uniform was the same, although we didn't wear the haversack on drill nights to save the material from wear and tear.

After inspection, we would perform a series of drill movements before breaking up for classes in First Aid, Signalling, Semaphore and Wayfaring. Gymnastics were performed at the school in Rupert Road on Wednesday night where Mr. Rushton would take the class from 7.30pm to 9pm. There was a very good band comprising eight bugles and six drums. Band practice being at 7.30pm on the Tuesday night.

For Sunday worship the older boys who had been confirmed were allowed to attend the Parish Church for the 10am Communion Service. Each Sunday there would be about forty boys at the service, all sitting together. For those of us not old enough to be confirmed, a Bible Class was held in the wooden hut behind the Parish Hall in Rupert Road at 10.30am. This was taken by Mr. Barlow who lived close by. Thursdays, there was a Seniors Club in the Parish rooms in Rupert Road for the over 16's.

I was interested in joining the band, and was given an old bugle to practice with. This drove mother mad, and I would come home each lunch time from school and spend about half an hour in our back bedroom learning the scales, and eventually learning marches. I was soon in the band and would eventually go on to become the proud possessor of the Silver Bugle and become Band Master.

We would parade to the Parish Church once a month and after Morning Service would march round the Parish before returning to St. Andrews Hall to be dismissed.

Christmas 1942 was spent in Alder Hey Hospital. I had been playing football at school in November and I collided with a goal post and damaged the right side of my neck just behind my ear. After visiting our local G.P. and having the new tablets called M&B's which were supposed to clear all ailments, I went to the hospital and was admitted. A visit to the local surgery at No. 1 Liverpool Road was to enter the home of the Jones family.

Part of the house was given over to the doctor who had the front room for his office, and another room for the waiting patients. Part of this room was the Jones dining room and was curtained off. Those waiting for the doctor would have the aroma of dinner floating through the curtain and many stomachs would rumble whilst waiting to go into the consulting room.

Inside you would find Dr. Abrams puffing a cigarette continuously whilst he made his examination. In the corner of the room was a small dispensary where he would make up a bottle of medicine in a few minutes. His fee, was usually 1/6d, plus the cost of the medicine. If he came to a sick person at home his fee was 2/6d. He would arrive in a Morris 8 saloon, still puffing on a cigarette. He had a bad heart and his hands were always blue with bad circulation.

The ward was mixed and the ages ranged from a few months to about 13 years. The wards were three storeys high and I was in the middle one. I was not allowed out of bed because I had a very high temperature, but as I was next to the sluice room I was able to slip out to the toilet. On Saturday afternoon a lady doctor came and said "We will have to put you to sleep and make a little cut in your neck, as there is an abscess which will not go away". She went away and came back with two nurses and another doctor who had a gauze mask which was put over my face and chloroform was dripped onto it to put me to sleep. When I woke up I had a thick bandage round my neck. I found out later that the operation was done in my bed because the doctor thought I was too sick to be taken to the theatre.

In the ward above were wounded soldiers. I remember lying in bed at night hearing them walking with crutches and sticks across the floor above me. I was kept in bed for about seven days. I was allowed up for a few hours each day. I was able to look out of the window onto the garden and drive ways and could see the wounded soldiers in their hospital blue uniforms, walking and sitting in the grounds.

The nurses, as in all hospitals, worked very hard and were

never allowed any rest time by the Ward Sister. One day we heard that one of our favourite nurses had become sick herself. We were told by the other nurses she would not be paid or be allowed food from the Nurses Home, so those patients who were allowed up would take some bread and butter and anything left from our meals and hide it until the Sister went off duty, then we would give our hidden meal to one of the nurses to take away when she went off duty to our sick nurse.

Just before Christmas, the nurses decorated the ward and on Christmas Eve they walked through all the wards, wearing their cloaks and carrying candles and singing carols. Overnight Father Christmas came round and each child received a present from the wounded soldiers above. Before being discharged, those of us able to get up were given little jobs to do, such as making up packs of swabs (little balls of cotton wool, taken from a large roll) the size of a table tennis ball. Gauze and lint dressings were made in various sizes. Each one had to be folded neatly, leaving no untidy edges. These dressings and swabs would be placed in a highly polished steel drum about 18" diameter and 12" deep. This drum had side clips that revealed perforated holes through which high pressure steam and then dry heat would be allowed through to sterilise the dressings. When the drum was full it was taken away with many others to the autoclave, a machine for sterilising the dressings. These drums would be returned to the wards and operating theatres for use afterwards.

We also had to rewind bandages after they had been washed in the laundry. We did this by holding a length of bandage before us, tucking the end under our chins and winding up as tight as possible, repeating the process until all the bandage was rewound. I was soon discharged, and after a short period of convalescence at home, returned to school after the Christmas holidays.

Cousin Harold, now about seven years old managed to get a little Saturday job. On either side of the house where he lived were Orthodox Jewish families. Each Saturday morning he would go to each house to clean out the fire grate and relay and light the coal fire. This was done by him because no Jew could perform any task on the Sabbath.

The school was now fourth in the city with our salvage collection which now averaged 95lb per head, for the previous six months.

Hit songs for 1942 were 'This is the Army, Mr. Jones', 'White Christmas' and 'We'll meet again'.

1943

The Yanks arrive at Dovecot

At the start of the new year, I was allowed to play out and visit other boy's homes. One particular friend at that time was Noel Fisher. He lived with his parents and elder brother on Liverpool Road, Huyton. We would play with Meccano, our Hornby trains and do jig saws.

I went with him one Sunday to visit his uncle and cousins in Wallasey. We went by tram to the Pier Head, then by Ferry boat to Seacombe. We then travelled on a yellow Wallasey Corporation bus to Liscard Village. His cousins were all girls and we were invited to stay for dinner and tea. We eventually started back for home about seven o'clock, catching the bus back to Seacombe. We arrived at the ferry just in time to see the boat sail for Liverpool, so had to wait for twenty minutes for the next one.

We caught a 10B tram for home and when we were at Green Lane, the tram caught fire! We then had to walk along Prescot Road to the tram sheds to wait for a tram to come out of the sheds to continue our journey.

When I arrived home I had to face a stern interrogation from dad, who was not entirely convinced about the fire.

On Thursday, 21st January the head assembled the whole school to give a talk on Hygiene, Speech and Manners. He said "Without personal hygiene, the body will not function properly, so you should all be aware of the consequences of not being clean". He also went on to talk about the correct use of English in speaking to the teachers and to other boys and the observance of correct ways of behaviour in and out of school. the practice and observance of these three factors would help in obtaining satisfactory employment after leaving school.

The following day P.C. Parry of Liverpool City Police gave an interesting lecture on 'Safety First'.

On Monday 8th February I was one of twenty boys selected to attend an Orchestral Concert at the Philharmonic Hall, Hope Street, given by the Philharmonic Orchestra under their Conductor, Dr. Malcom Sargent.

None of us had ever been to a concert before and we were a little apprehensive about going. Mrs Leather the teacher in charge of us told us it would be like going to the cinema. We were given tram tickets from the school office and set off to travel on the 40 tram to Brownlow Hill. We then walked along Hope Street to the Concert Hall.

As we were early arriving, we were able to sit at the front of the stalls. Soon the hall was full of children from schools from many parts of Liverpool.

The Orchestra filed in and took their places on the stage. Dr. Sargent walked on to the platform and the orchestra stood up. After acknowledging the applause of the audience, the musicians sat down on the wave of the conductor's baton. Dr. Sargent began by introducing the various parts of the orchestra, strings, woodwind, brass and percussion, who he introduced as the 'The Odd Job Department' as they were called upon to play a variety of instruments. Each section in turn played a piece of music then the whole orchestra was brought together to play a complete piece.

The highlight of the afternoon was a performance of Handel's 'Water Music'. This music was written for a party given by King George I on the river Thames in 1715. Dr. Sargent told the story that Handel was the King's Master of Music, but he had fallen out of favour. The music was written in an effort to try to heal the differences between them. There are nine parts to the while piece and we were introduced to each section before the orchestra played the complete work.

The Air, we were told, was written to ask the King's forgiveness, paraphrasing the words 'Please be kind to me'. Those who know the music will be familiar with the refrain. After this party the King did restore Handel to his position, doubling his salary in the process. After the concert, we were allowed to make our own way home. I walked to the Pier Head to catch a tram, after looking in the shop windows on the way.

Monday 22nd saw the start of 'America Week'. Various activities were planned and on Wednesday we had an hours programme of music. On Friday Mr. Price took twenty five boys to the Picton Hall to hear a song recital by Mr. Roy Henderson.

The head had to go to Broadgreen Hospital for an X-ray on his ankle. A dog had run into the front wheel of his bicycle on his way to school that morning causing him to fall into the road.

Playing out after tea with the other girls and boys was an adventure. A group of us would meet on the corner of Woolfall Heath Avenue, and as there was still a blackout, would play hide and seek and other games, hiding in the gardens and up side paths. One 'Game' we were notorious for, was to collect the waste food bins that were at the end of many roads, empty their contents into one so that is was overflowing, take it very carefully to a pre-selected house, lean it against the front door, knock loudly on the knocker and run. When the front door was opened, all the smelly vegetable peelings and tea leaves would spill out into the hallway. There would usually be a loud exclamation of outrage and we would get a mouthful of threats like "I know who yer are, I'll tell yer dad when I clean up this mess".

There was great excitement at school on Wednesday the 24th March. Our first Wireless and moveable speaker was delivered. This equipment was kept in the Head's office and was wheeled out by his prefects under supervision of one of the members of staff, to the classroom that had been specially prepared for radio broadcasts.

Tuesday the 6th April saw us have a visit from Major Green and Lieutenant Gabb of the U.S.A.A.F., together with Councillor

Boothman as guests of the assembled boys' and girls' schools. I had been selected to go in B.B. uniform with a girl who was in the Girl Guides, to meet the visitors who were to come via East Prescot Road to Dovecot shops, from where we were to direct them to the school. After we had been waiting for some time, we decided to return to school to find the programme that had been arranged by Miss Campbell, the Girls' Head Teacher was almost over. Our guests had arrived by another way.

The programme had begun with an introduction by Miss Campbell, after which the boys and girls had sung two songs 'Pioneers' and 'America the Beautiful'. Mr. Clarke then welcomed the visitors. The Two American Officers addressed the children, after which they invited questions from the assembly.

A vote of Thanks was given by Edna Ford and Frederick Cave. There was then a parade of boys and girls in uniform. The afternoon was declared "A very pleasant and inspiring occasion".

Monday the 13th April saw two boys being implicated in the theft (borrowing) of tools from the woodwork room. They were interviewed by detectives and were found to be involved in housebreaking. Some property was recovered from their homes. They were later to appear in court on the 18th April.

A further loudspeaker was purchased on the 15th from Messrs Coombe & Sons, Worcester, on the advice of a representative of the B.B.C On the 4th of May the sum of £14 15s 2d. was subscribed by the boys for the purchase of a second wireless. The whole school assembled on Thursday the 6th to hear a broadcast about Russia. This programme lasted twenty minutes. The following week a similar broadcast was heard and afterwards news of the African Campaign was read to the school.

Our target of £180 for National Savings was received on the 19th and on the following day, news of the appearance in Court of the two boys accused of theft was received. One was sent to a remand home for one week and the other put on probation. Salvage collection rose to 7350 lbs. for one week.

On Friday the 28th, the school was given a half day holiday in appreciation of the amount collected by Liverpool schools during 'Wings of Victory' week.

At Boys' Brigade we paraded on the Saturday of 'Wings of Victory' week. A Spitfire cost £5,000, and a Lancaster Bomber £15,000. Marching along Dinas Lane, Ashover Avenue, East Prescot Road and Dovecot Avenue, to Pilch Lane. Here we joined the main parade of Civil Defence, Fire Service, Home Guard, A.T.C., Army and Navy Cadets, Scouts, Guides, St. John Ambulance and Red Cross detachments. After the parade we made our way back to St. Andrew's hall via Page Moss Lane and Dinas Lane.

Sporting Activities continued at school with a Swimming Gala held on the 17th June at the Harold Davies Swimming Baths, East Prescot Road. At the end of the proceedings the Head gave a closing speech and said "The normal staff of this department has always worked as a team in the common bond of loyalty to the school, and I am glad to record, with deep appreciation, the fact that these teachers who have joined us during the absence if nine of our original staff on War service, have become similarly embued with this team spirit. In this tribute to them I must include the only two remaining members of the pre-war staff, Mr. Winter and Mr. Free, who have so successfully played their part and have so obviously infected the newcomers with the school idea of Loyalty and Service". A profit of £8.2s.2d. was made on the night!

The school Annual Sports Day was held on Tuesday the 23rd. The Trophy was won by Childwall House.

The following Tuesday, the school was visited by a Miss Hooker who gave a lecture on Poland. This was accompanied by Lantern slides, and was very interesting and instructive. On 16th July a white paper on Post War Education advocated free schooling up to the age of 16.

During the holidays I managed to open dad's 'Holy of Holies', his tool box. Inside were all manner of tools, but what took my eye was a round object, wrapped in oiled cloth. On unwrapping it

LIVERPOOL WINGS FOR VICTORY WEEK.

No. **171**

Liverpool, 15th May. 1943.

RECEIVED with cordial thanks from: Ruth Bassnett, 16 Dawson Grove L'pool 5.

the sum of One Pounds,

Five Shillings and Pence,

being a free gift to the campaign.

£ 1 : 5 : -

signature Hon. Treasurer.

THE LORD MAYOR GREATLY APPRECIATES YOUR SUPPORT.

Ruth Bassnett, aged 8 years, raffled a kitchen scrubbing brush, selling 300 tickets at one penny each to raise the sum of £1-5/- in aid of the Liverpool Wings for Victory Week May 1943.

I found a brand new Cricket ball. Vernon and I went out into the back garden to have a game of Cricket with my new 'find'. He had the bat and I had the ball. I soon got the hang of bowling with this ball, but unfortunately Vernon couldn't get bat on ball, which went crashing through the livingroom window. Mum came out and took the bat off Vernon and took the ball from the livingroom floor, then put them away with the words many mothers have said to their children "Wait till your dad gets home". Wait I did. When he finally came home, mum told him about my opening his tool box, finding the cricket ball and breaking the window. After a 'severe talking to' dad finished with these words "Any further misbehaviour from you, I'll separate your body from your breath".

At Boys' Brigade, we held our annual camp of 10 days duration at Castle Park Farm, Ruthin. We always were at camp for the August Bank holiday, which was the first Monday in the month. A previous Curate at Roby Parish Church, Rev. Bartlett had become Vicar of All Saints, Princes Park, where there was a Scout Troop. The two Vicars would go looking for camp sites, usually in February, which would be booked for four weeks, with the Scouts having the first use of the site before we took it over.

This was my first camp and the cost of £1.10s. included train fare from Birkenhead to Ruthin. This was the first time I had been away from home by myself, and was quite an adventure. We left at 7am. on the Wednesday morning and travelled by tram to the Pier Head and then by Ferry to Birkenhead where we were to travel on the 8.30am. train to Chester, but due to troop movements, this train was cancelled, and we had to wait until about mid-day before another train was available. We eventually arrived at Ruthin about 5pm. and had to walk about a mile to the camp site. All our tents were already pitched and all we had to do was go to the farm yard to fill our sleeping sacks with straw (no Lilo's in those days). We always sent an advance party the previous day to lay out the site and clean up after the Scouts. They seemed to be more interested in building Rope Bridges across the river than keeping the site clean!

After being allocated our sleeping space in the tent, the Corporal in charge would line us all up and we were ready for a meal. Although all food was rationed, being in the country was like being in another world! We had a cooked breakfast every morning with fresh eggs and there was always plenty of meat at dinner time. A typical day would start with Reveille at 7.30am. wash and make up bed space for 8am, when we would be taken on a run of about a mile to the town park, where we would do physical exercises for about 15 minutes, followed by a run back to camp for breakfast which usually consisted of corn flakes or porridge, followed by something fried, bread and jam and tea.

When all was finished the camp would parade for tent inspection, when the Orderly Officer would inspect the kit laid out, soap, toothbrush, toothpaste, towel and the area immediately surrounding the tent, as well as the boys on parade. Then there would be morning prayers and the raising of the Union Jack. Then games would take us to dinner at 1pm. Each tent had to do a day of Fatigues, that is, cleaning the cooking dishes and dixies, preparing vegetables, buttering bread and generally keeping everything clean. When on your days fatigues it was not always possible to leave the camp site.

After dinner, which was always followed by a pudding, we were allowed to go up to the town, where we would spend a little of our pocket money. There was a camp bank run by one of the Officers, who would have a bag of money. We would have a Bank card showing how much we had saved and the withdrawals made. Tea was at 5pm. which was usually salad and cake, with bread and jam. Afterwards we could return to the town or play cricket of football until 9pm. when it was supper time. This consisted of a mug of cocoa and a slice of bread and jam eaten round the camp fire. After supper Dickie Jarvis who was very good at telling ghost stories, would start. He would have the younger members enthralled with his story, then he would stop, just before he reached the most chilling part and would say "I'll finish if off tomorrow night". At 9.30pm. the camp would parade for the ceremony of Retreat, when evening prayers would be said and the Flag would be lowered. Lights out was at 10pm.

My first encounter with the enemy face to face was when one of the Italian prisoners of war, working of the farm, came over to the camp fire one evening, bringing with him a Concertina. He played and sang songs from Italy. We were a little shy of him at first, but soon got to know him quite well. From memory, his name was Antonio.

The previous year the camp had been inspected by Field Marshall Lord Gort, who had been commander of the British forces in France, just prior to the evacuation at Dunkirk. His headquarters were in Ruthin Castle and he had seen the boys in the town and heard the band when they practised in the field close to the castle.

On Tuesday 31st August, I, along with four other boys of my year at school went to the Liverpool City College of Art to sit an examination for an Industrial Art Scholarship. The examination was based on Maths, English, General Knowledge and Art.

At the start of September the Ministry of Food declared a shortage of helpers to bring in the harvest. Farm camps were set up and Civil servants were given an extra weeks leave to go and help in the fields.

The B.B.C. broadcast a service to the nation on Friday, 3rd of September on the fourth anniversary of the outbreak of War. Both departments assembled in the school hall to listen. Reception was excellent and the service was very impressive.

A lady who lived in Page Moss Lane came to school on Monday the 6th to complain about stones being thrown over her wall into her garden and damaging her poultry house and breaking her kitchen window. This damage was done after normal school hours, but in play centre time. The head offered to look into the problem.

On Monday the 9th it was announced that Italy had surrendered the previous day to General Eisenhower. This was marked by a short service that was held on the veranda around the Western lawn, led by Mr. Clark.

We stood to attention as the Union Jack was hoisted and we sang the National Anthem. Mr. Clark said "We should show a spirit of thankfulness not boastfulness at this victory. This event marks a stage in the struggle for victory which we will achieve". We sang the hymn 'Now thank we all our God', a prayer for peace was read, the Collect for peace was said followed by the Lord's Prayer, and the Benediction. The service concluded with the singing of the 'Song for Liberty'. The assembled pupils then marched past the Flag to dismiss to their classes.

The school was given a grant of £10 to set up a printing press on Friday the 10th. An Arab Platen press was obtained together with two type frames containing various founts of type, together with other printing furniture. This equipment was housed in the Woodwork department.

There was a sudden drop in attendance this day due to stomach pains and sickness. Of those who attended, several were sent home.

Tuesday the 21st saw a surprise visit of the school Nurse. She found three boys suffering from Scabies and seven with Nits.

On Tuesday 5th October we were visited by Miss Hayward, B.B.C. Education Officer and Mr. Lloyd. they found class 2B listening to the B.B.C.'s 'European heritage' series. Friday the 26th saw a visit if six Polish Scouts and two Girl Guides who gave a talk to both departments. An Epidiascope was used to show views of the Polish countryside and cities.

When we arrived at school on Thursday 4th November, the tree outside the teachers' entrance had been destroyed during the night by vandals.

Armistice Day, November 11th was observed by an assembly of both departments, with boys and girls in youth organisation uniform. We listened to a broadcast address given by General Smuts of South Africa. Thursday the 25th brought a visit from Chaplain Bates of the U.S. Army to address both departments and to answer questions.

On Wednesday 1st December there was a serious complaint about the days Pudding and on the following Monday, Mice remains and Weevils were found in the dinner. Samples were sent by office messenger for inspection by a Food Inspector.

The temperature in the classrooms was dropping and on Monday 13th December reached a low of 42 degrees Fahrenheit. We carried on with our lessons wearing our coats to keep us warm. Before the school broke up for the Christmas holiday the Head commenced reading 'A Christmas Carol' by Charles Dickens, to the whole school. These readings were carried on until the Christmas party. We started the Christmas holiday on Tuesday the 21st.

Aunt Gladys and cousin Harold had now moved to Greenbank Road, where they had as their next-door neighbour, Miss Avril Angers, a well-known radio personality and Comedienne. Harold had moved schools and was now at Dovedale Road. John and Philip were still evacuated to North Wales.

The hit songs for 1943 were 'You'll Never Know', 'Brazil' and 'My Heart and I'.

1944

I Go to Work - then back to School!

January 4th saw Hitler ordering the mobilisation of all children over the age of ten years.

We returned to school to cold classrooms as there was little coke to heat the water of the central heating system. Our Evening Institute classes continued and plays and other entertainments were put on in the main hall.

The Government announced on 17th February that increased attention was being attached to Post-War conditions. It announced plans for a National Health Service with the countrys full resources being used to promote good health for all citizens. This will mean a free and comprehensive medical service as soon as possible. It would cost £148 million a year to run.

The school leaving age would be raised to fifteen later this year and then, after some years, to sixteen. There will be three types of free secondary education without a means test:- Grammar, Secondary Modern and Technical. At the beginning of each school day there will be a compulsory act of non-denominational collective worship. Local authorities will be under obligation to provide school playing fields, gymnasium and swimming baths.

The B.B.C. announces it will develop schools radio to accompany the new education system being planned.

In Germany, boy soldiers fifteen years old have been found in some front line units.

On Monday the 28th Ralph Woods aged fourteen and Thomas

Clare, fifteen, were taken to the Northern Hospital, Taggart Avenue after being seriously hurt when, with three other boys who were killed by the explosion of a mortar bomb which they had been playing with.

The three boys who died were David Nixon sixteen, Dennis Urmson fifteen and his brother Raymond thirteen. All lived in Adcote Road. Two other boys who ran behind trees when their playmates picked up the bomb near an old anti-aircraft gun site in Childwall Valley Road, escaped injury. The funerals of the three boys killed took place on Wednesday 3rd March at the church of the Holy Spirit, Dovecot. On the following day one of the seriously injured boys died and his funeral took place at the same church on Monday 6th March.

The whole school was shocked by this tragic happening, my brother especially as he was very friendly with Raymond Urmson.

Education Minister R.A. Butler announces the ban on women teachers marrying will be lifted because of their great war effort. Later in the month M.P.'s voted to give women teachers the same pay as men.

My time as Senior Prefect was coming to an end as I was due to leave school at the end of the current term. I had been appointed Appearance Prefect back in August 1943. My duties consisted of inspecting all classes as they marched into assembly each morning, pulling out the boys who had dirty shoes or boots.

I had an assistant who inspected the other line. Mr. Elliott had made a shoe shine box complete with brushes, polish and a polishing cloth. Each boy pulled out would have his name taken and would be charged a half-penny to use the cleaning materials. If a boy's name appeared in my book three times in one week he would be listed for punishment and would have to report to Mr Free to receive sentence. This usually meant having 'Stripes' recorded against his 'House'. Persistent offending received the cane. On Friday morning I would go round the school collecting the fines then go to the local hardware shop to purchase fresh supplies of polish. Any surplus money was taken to the Head's office to be put in the general fund.

The week before leaving school I was informed that I had been successful in obtaining an Industrial Art Scholarship to the Liverpool City School of Art, starting in September. As dad earned over £3 per week, he was asked to make a one-off payment of £3 to the Education Committee. Between April and September I was persuaded by dad to find employment. I applied for, and was successful in gaining a position as Office Junior with a firm of Solicitors, Messrs. Radcliffe-Smith, Abercrombie & Co., 14 Cook Street, Liverpool 2. My duties included dusting the office before the Articled Clerk, Mr. Mullen, arrived promptly at 9.15, delivering mail by hand to other city centre businesses, a job taught me by the Junior Clerk, who was waiting for his call-up papers. The delivering of mail was an experience and on a wet day was an adventure to find the driest way to such places as the Corn Exchange or as far as Edmund Street. There was also the shopping to be done for Mr. Abercrombie's secretary. I soon learned the diversity of the term 'Professional Advice'. One day a client telephoned for advice as to what she should plant in her garden, as her gardener had been called up. Mr. Mullen gave her a list of flowers and shrubs she could plant. When she had gone off the telephone I was instructed to enter in the Account book Mrs. Smith to professional advice £5. I had to go to the Bank of England, which was on the corner of Castle Street and Cook Street, to pay money into a special account of Mr. Abercrombie. On entering the Bank there were two men in pink coats and top hats waiting to usher your through the doors to the cashiers. When leaving the Bank they would hold open the doors to the street for the customers to leave.

Another time I was taken with Mr. Mullen to a large house in the Sandfield Park area to be a witness to a will. We were taken by chauffeur driven car from the office and when we arrived, were served afternoon tea by a maid. Afterwards the Will was brought out for signing and witnessed. Then I was given 30/- as my witness fee, and ushered out to find my own way home.

Mr. Abercrombie was quite old, his son was a Major in the Army in Africa and he would occasionally tell the assembled staff of his exploits. I tried to find out who Radcliffe-Smith was but without much success.

The copying of letters was done by using a carbon cloth which was soaked in water, wrung almost dry and placed on the letter. On top of this was placed a plain sheet of paper and when the days correspondence was complete, all the letters and carbon cloths were placed in a bookbinders press for about ten minutes to effect the transfer of words from the original to the plain paper to give a copy. Then the originals would be placed in their envelopes ready for posting. The duplicates were then ready for filing away. It was my job, in my own time, to take the post to the Post Office in India Buildings on my way home.

D Day came on the 6th of June. The news was brought into the office by Mr. Abercrombie's secretary, who used to arrive at 9.30am each morning. She had heard it on her way to the office. It was amazing to see the change of expressions on the faces of the people in the city. Everybody was talking about how soon the War would be over.

It was our Boys' Brigade display on the same night. The Company being so large, had to give two performances as the church hall had limited accommodation for our families and friends. At the end of our performance, after badges and certificates had been awarded, came the time for promotions. As usual there were a number of boys wanting their first step up the ladder of command. With the number of members in the Company at the time we were allowed four each or Staff Sergeants, Sergeants and Corporals all promoted over the previous years. The junior rank of Lance Corporal being the first step up the promotion ladder. There were about twenty boys eligible for this promotion through length of service, attendance both during the week and on Sunday, the number of badge classes attended and conduct. I was one of the four lucky lads given the first stripe that night! Earlier

I had been awarded the National Service Badge. This was earned by doing one hundred hours of voluntary service to assist the War effort. I completed my one hundred hours by collecting salvage at school, collecting from the local shops paper, cardboard, wooden boxes, string - in fact anything that could be re-used. I did this collection with Stan Blundell three mornings a week. Next came my First Aid Badge. This badge took two years to obtain. The first year a certificate was awarded. The Buglers Badge came next. For this you had to play fifteen military calls from the Army manual. Then the three year service Anchor and the one year star, or as we called it the 'pip'. This was awarded to every boy who had been absent less than twice during the session from either Drill Parade or Sunday Bible Class.

Our office was in a building next to Henstocks the Stationers. One morning I was asked to go to the shop for a map of the uncharted areas of the South Pacific. Waiting impatiently in the queue in the shop, I had a nagging feeling that everything was not quite right. Just as I was about to ask for the map the penny dropped and I ordered a dozen HB pencils to be added to our account. Back at the office I told them that the map was on order.

The first V1 Rocket attacks took place on the South of England on the 15th of July. This caused mothers and children to be evacuated again to the West of England.

Our annual camp was held again at Castle Park Farm, Ruthin. At this camp I was second-in-command to Norman Bowes of a tent. He, like me was in the band, playing a bugle. The scouts had been there before us and had been unlucky with the weather.

On August Bank Holiday Monday the local farmers were holding a Sheepdog Trial. One of our Cooks, Mr. Fred Bowler decided that he would dress up and spend the afternoon watching the dogs perform. After dinner he washed and changed into his best blue serge suit and was ready to go, when he saw a Fatigue party cleaning a Dixie that had been used for making custard in. They were not making a very good of it, so he went over to show them the correct way to clean it. In the process he got soot on his hands, so decided to go through the bushes to the river to wash them. Our other Cook, Mr. Ted Pinnington then comes on the scene, sees the Dixie half full of dirty water, picks it up and throws the water over the bushes. Unfortunately poor Fred got the lot all over his best suit. Spluttering and shouting, he emerged from the bushes to be met by Ted, who, consoling him, wiped him down with a dirty oven cloth! Poor old Fred never did get to the Sheepdog trial. We had a flying visit from some of our old boys who were home on leave from the forces. Some of them had taken part in the D Day landings. They didn't say much about their experiences they were just glad to be home amongst the people they knew.

During this camp the farmer had cause to complain about one boy who had been riding on the back of his prize bull. Sergeant Alfie Jones was the culprit and the Captain was very close to reducing him to the rank of private and sending him home. Later Alfie was one of the last to be killed by enemy action in Europe.

While we were at camp, PLUTO (Pipe Line Under the Ocean), originated at Dingle Oil Jetty, began pumping oil from the Isle of Wight to Cherburg on Saturday 12th August.

General Montgomery was appointed Field Marshall by the King at a ceremony at Buckingham Palace on Thursday the 31st.

My return to full time education started on the 6th of September. As well as the Printing students there were Art students. They were given preferential treatment over us, as they had first choice at lunch time, leaving us to have what they didn't like. There were two bells rung for lunch. The first was for the Art classes and the second for the Printers. This was to help the canteen staff cope with the number of students wanting a meal. The students in the Printing class were to study English, Maths, Geography, Heraldry, Letterpress and Lithographic printing, hand composition and Art.

Names I can remember from the class are:- Bob Edwards, with whom I was to serve apprenticeship with later, Derek Johanson, Clive Yates, Carter (regarded by us as teachers pet) Greeba, Nickson, Stonier, Devine, Devereaux and John Yates (no relation

Fred Bowler, Ted Pinnington and Tom Hunt cooking dinner, Castle Park Farm, Ruthin, August 1943.

to Clive). John had to leave the course at the end of the first year due to the death of his father of a heart attack whilst on duty with the Liverpool City Police. His mother needed him to go to work to help support the rest of the family. He was found an apprenticeship as a Machine Minder.

Our Art teacher was Mr. Irwin Weisner, who came from the Czechoslovak city of Brno. He was a little man with steel grey hair and gold rimmed spectacles. He would teach us for ten hours a week. When he thought you were working well, he would reward you by sending you off for a walk, two at at time.

One day it was my turn, so with another boy, we went out of the main entrance into Hope Street. Just as we were going to cross the road I saw a piece of paper lying in the gutter. On closer examination it turned out to be two ten shilling notes lying on the ground. As there was nobody about, we had one each.

Mr. Weisner was fond of Aesops Fables, so he would read them to us. At the end of the story he would say "Now boys you will draw" meaning we had to interpret the story in a drawing. All classes had a 'hard lad'. We had one by the name of Nickson. He would rub poor Mr. Weisner up the wrong way until one day, when he had been particularly obnoxious, Mr. Weisner called him out to the front of the class and said "Nickson, you think you know bugger all, but you know bugger nozzings". After this verbal attack, our 'hard lad' was a changed pupil.

Mr. Gardner was the teacher of Heraldry. Why we had to learn that subject was beyond us! We wanted to be printers not Heralds. His class was from 2 to 4pm every Tuesday. Before this we would have English with Mrs. Dodd. Her husband was in the Army, and after setting us to work, she would spend the rest of the lesson knitting sweaters and socks to send to him. We also found out that she could not stand a cat near her. One day we decided to round up all the cats we could find in the college basement. I think we found three and these were placed in her desk, which had a lift-up top. the cats took an instant dislike both to the desk top and to each other and started to make a noise. Mrs. Dodd came into the room, heard the noise in the desk, lifted the lid and the cats leapt out onto her. She screamed so loud she was heard all over the college and we were almost expelled on the spot by the Principal, who came to investigate the commotion.

We would have a ten minute break after this lesson to go to the toilet and prepare for Mr. Gardner. However, quite a few of us would develop headaches or find we had very bad stomach pains or toothache and would rapidly disappear along Mount Street and home.

We were eventually caught and were called to the College Principal's office. Mr. Hugill, the Principal, was not impressed by our excuses and we were given a punishment of 200 lines to be written on Poster paper, which we had to buy from the College shop. When we presented our work to him he almost exploded! He wanted us to write the sentence with a brush - something we had no experience of!

Our introduction to Hand Composing came one Monday morning when the class had to assemble in the Lecture Theatre. The teacher for this subject was Mr. Peter Malone, reputed to have been a goalkeeper with Liverpool F.C. many years previously.

We had to write reams of notes and the first words to be written on this subject were 'Find a Frame in a Good Light'. The frame referred to is a piece of printing furniture containing cases of type which had a sloping top and carried a further case of type from which compositors would set each individual character into a setting stick.

It is hard to imagine a first year apprentice going into a Composing room and saying to the Foreman "I want a frame in a good light". A kick in a certain part of his anatomy would have been the reply!

September 17th was declared the end of the complete blackout with what was called a "Partial Dim-Out". This enabled vehicles to show more light at night.

At college our teacher of Lithography was Mr. Cope, a man

with absolutely no sense of humour. We were taught the rudiments of this very absorbing subject, being taught to grain plates so that they could be used again with a different subject printed on them.

We made fine line copper engravings with Nitric Acid and Wax, used a Gallery Camera to make a negative. The exposure of the film was determined by the removal and replacement of a lens cap on the front of the camera, counting the time from a clock on the wall. A shutter would be pulled down at the back of the camera, so sealing out the light from the sheet of film. The box was then lifted off the camera and taken into a dark room to be developed.

Letterpresss Printing was taught by Mr. Tom Fleming, who had been a very fine craftsman before he had turned to teaching. He was, unfortunately, deaf, and we boys were not very kind to him at times. As I mentioned earlier, there were two bells for lunch and during the morning lesson we had with him, one of the class would call out "The first bell is ringing Sir" and when the first bell really did ring, another would call out "Second bell's ringing Sir". He would then dismiss the class early so that we could be first in the queue for lunch. He taught us machine printing, the different kinds of paper used, and the mixing of different colours of ink. He also introduced us to what was called 'Make Ready'. This is the process of making a perfect printed sheet that has no faint areas or type that was too heavy, marking the paper so that the letters could be felt through the paper.

He arranged for us to have a football team and set up matches for us to play on a Saturday morning in Newsham Park. In the summer he helped to form a cricket team.

We also attended the Gymnasium in Mount Street. The Instructor there was Mr. Charles Lord, a former participant in the 1936 Olympic Games as a Gymnast. He was a great admirer of the American Sprinter Jesse Owens, who beat the best Hitler could find in the Sprints. Mr. Lord was a little man, strong as an Ox. He could climb a rope with one hand and could stand on his head without using his hands to steady himself. He liked us to play a Danish game called Kaptain Ball. This was similar to Hand-ball, except a goal was scored by throwing the ball to the goal keeper. A goal guard stood in front of the keeper to try to stop the keeper catching the ball. We would play to the rules for part of the time, then he would shout "All in", and the rules were forgotten.

Armistice Sunday this year held a special significance for our Company as we paraded to the Parish Church. For the first time we were remembering boys we had known and who had made the supreme sacrifice on the field of battle. I was to sound the Last Post and Reveille during the service.

At the end of November I was confirmed at Huyton Parish Church, with twenty other girls and boys from Roby Parish. Each year the annual Confirmation Service was held at either Huyton or Roby. Other churches in the area also sent their candidates to the service which was conducted by the Bishop of Liverpool.

At the end of term the college had a Christmas party where all the students joined together in a night of fun and games which went on until the early hours of the following day.

My first Christmas Communions was at Roby Parish Church, commencing at 11.45pm. After the Service the boys and girls went for a walk along Roby Road and up to Huyton Village, then along Rupert Road where we went our different ways home. I arrived home at about 2.30am. Mum was still up, waiting for me to return. Christmas day was a time of eating and eating again. Turkey was on the menu this year and mum had prepared her own recipe for the stuffing that smelled so good from the oven.

We had sprouts, carrot and turnip, boiled and roast potatoes and lots of gravy. Christmas pudding followed and to finish the festive meal, a cup of coffee. This was a rare treat for Vernon and I as coffee was not in plentiful supply.

Tea time brought mum's sisters to tea. They would arrive about six o'clock bringing presents for us all. Tea would consist of salad, tinned meat, tinned fruit and evaporated milk, Christmas

Cake and mince pies. Our 'Points' would have been saved up over a long period to provide such a spread.

Afterwards we would play games such as Snakes and Ladders or Draughts before it was time to see our guests to the tram stop for the last tram home.

The popular hit songs of 1944 were:- 'There goes that Song again' and `Mairzy Doats'.

1945

It's all over!

On the 15th of January, the first Boat Train for five years left London for the Continent, and on the 20th Mr. Butler says "The State will pay 55% of the cost of the new education system".

At home, I regularly attended the Sunday Communion Service at the Parish Church, along with about forty other boys. We would sit four to a pew and when it was our turn to receive Communion, the boy sitting nearest to the aisle would stand and step out, take three paces back and wait for the second boy to stand into the aisle, who took two paces back. The third boy would carry out the same manoeuvre, followed by the fourth boy who would march straight out and up the aisle, followed by the other three. This enabled us to return to our places without having to disturb the other Communicants.

After the Service I would sometimes ride my bicycle to Sefton Park and on the way back visit Aunt Laura and Uncle George. Laura was one of dad's sisters and lived in Bowland Avenue. She and George had a son also named Ken. He was in the R.A.F. and had a very pretty girlfriend named Chris, who was in the A.T.S. They both looked very smart in their uniforms.

The youngest of dad's family, Leslie, was a prisoner of the Japanese in a camp in the North of Japan. Later my Sundays developed into a regular pattern. After attending Church, I would go home and then ride my bike to Moss Grove to visit my Aunts.

Arriving at number 27 and ringing the bell, I waited until a ritual that repeated itself every time there were visitors on a Sunday was carried out. The floors downstairs would have been scrubbed, carpets would have been taken out into the yard, hung over the washing line and beaten with a carpet beater. The damp floors would have newspaper laid on them to keep footprints away.

When the doorbell rang, one of the Aunts would go into the sitting room and peep through the curtains to see who was ringing, whilst another would be hurriedly picking up the newspapers and putting them behind the cellar door. Then one of them would open the door with a surprised look on her face and greet you with "Oh hello, we thought we heard the bell, come in".

I would do the odd jobs for them like swilling the yard and wash house. After dinner I would sometimes go to Lime Grove to visit my other Grandparents and Uncle Bill, dad's eldest brother. I would return to Moss Grove for tea before riding home to prepare for college the following morning.

I was introduced to Opera by Aunt Leah. She had a collection of records which she would play on a Gramophone which was made of beautiful grey-coloured wood. It had inlaid blue and gold flowers at the front corners just below the lid. I believe it was originally made in America.

These records were played with Fibre needles which could be re-sharpened with a device similar to a pencil sharpener. Her favourite singer was the Italian Tenor Beniamino Gigli. When the records were brought out, she would tell the story of the Opera before playing the piece.

We continued at college to be introduced to the mysteries or Printing. In the Composing Department we were shown the workings of the Monotype Keyboard and Caster, one of the earliest methods of computer typesetting.

The keyboard consisted of four banks of keys, one each for Roman, Bold, Italic and Small Capitals. The justification of lines of type was done by reading figures on what was known as the Justification Drum, similar in size to a tin of baked beans. When depressing a key on the keyboard, two metal rods would punch holes in a reel of paper about three inches wide. The holes

My Tent, Corwen Camp, August 1945. Ken Blashery, *far left* and Len Hunt, *far right*, other boys not known.

punched would be driven across the bridge of the Caster by compressed air and the die case which held the letters of the alphabet, figures and other symbols, would move in its frame over the nozzle of the pump that was primed with molten type metal. The metal forced into the die case would form the character which would cool very quickly and be pushed out by a rod to wait for the next letter.

One day Mr. Malone, who had been out for a liquid lunch, decided that some of the type cases used for hand setting were running short of letters, so our class was to run the Caster. In placing the pump nozzle into position, he forgot to secure the pump handle. I was given the job of starting the machine, he punched the holes in the paper on the bridge and instructed me to engage the pump. This I did, only to be showered with molten metal, some of which ran down my right arm, leaving a white scar, which took many years to disappear. It took the rest of the lesson to clear up the metal from the machine and the surrounding equipment.

On the 18th March all schools and universities in Japan were closed and everyone over the age of six was ordered to do war work.

In the Letterpress lesson, teachers pet called Carter informed Mr. Fleming about something that was going on between some of the boys at the back of the class. They were reprimanded, but they later had their revenge on poor little Carter, as they took him down to the cellar and hung him up on a nail by his braces, leaving him there for the whole of the next lesson.

We went to Cornwallis Street Baths about once a month instead of going to Pleasant Street Gymnasium.

In our Art lessons we were sometimes taken out by Mr. Weisner to draw buildings he found of interest to him. One day we were in Nile Street and he was extolling the beauty of a gable end of a house when the occupant, who was a very large man came over to him and demanded to know what we were all doing by spying on him and his family. A hasty retreat was made from

Helen Davies, *centre*, with Mai Jones *right* and Venice Roberts on *left*, in Corwen High Street, August 1945.

that end of the street.

We found another doorway of interest to him at the other end of the street, it had two columns supporting a canopy and had five steps up to the door. A little girl was sitting on the top step and when she saw twenty boys watching her, she lifted up her dress to reveal bare skin, had a pee and ran inside. Needless to say we all fell about laughing, so that ended the lesson for the day!

Other excursions took place to St. James' Cemetery to draw the tombs and gravestones and a memorable visit to the Scottish Church in Rodney Street, when twenty boys left the college and only about six arrived at the church. The rest of us got lost and went home.

April saw the partial blackout come to an end on the 23rd and on the 28th Mussolini the Italian Dictator was shot and hung by his feet, together with an aide and his Mistress, in Milan.

The following day the War was over in Italy, with the German and Italian Fascist Armies surrendering to Field Marshall Alexander. On the 30th, Grand Admiral Karl Doenitz, who had been certified in Manchester as Insane was named by Hitler as his successor.

The start of May saw the capture of Field Marshall Von Rundstedt, whilst Doenitz declared himself Fuhrer. Headlines in the Liverpool Echo for Thursday the 3rd declared `German retreat reaches tremendous Proportions. Monty links up with the Reds'. On the 4th there was a picture of a German Officer with a company of German Youth soldiers, aged from thirteen to sixteen years old. The back page headline declared 'Surrender at any Time'.

The following night the headline stated that 'four million Germans had been taken Prisoner and more than a million were to follow'. There were pictures of an historic meeting between representatives of Admiral Doenitz and Montgomery at his headquarters.

At 3am. on Monday the 7th there was a loud knocking on our front door. Dad got up and went down to see who was knocking.

It was our next-door neighbour, Mr. Joe Moss. He was a very light sleeper and also a keen radio listener. He had a huge radio console which could pick up stations all over the world. He had come to tell us that the War was over as he had picked up a broadcast that the German Army had surrendered unconditionally. He also wanted me to get up and go into his garden where he had a flagpole that carried his aerial for the radio. There he was going to raise the Union Jack and wanted me to play the General Salute on my bugle. Dad persuaded him that it was not a good idea at 3am in the morning. When the news was broadcast later by the B.B.C., there were wild scenes of jubilation everywhere. The Echo that night had banner headlines declaring 'War in Europe is over. Dramatic Announcement from Allied H.Q.'.

That night, along with other boys from B.B., I went round the roads where everybody was out laughing and singing. We were invited in to houses where impromptu parties were in full swing. We eventually arrived at Grovehurst Avenue where, in the middle there is a large square. A bonfire had been lit and anything and almost everything had been brought out to feed the flames. One lady shouted out when she saw a back gate being thrown onto the flames, 'Someone will have to explain that one to the 'Corpy' in the morning'. To which a reply came from the crowd 'Yes missus - it's yours'. I eventually got home about 2.30am too excited to sleep.

The 8th of May, VE Day as it was now called saw the arrangement of a ceremony to be held in Berlin, when Keitl would sign the Surrender Document in the Capital.

As the nights were now lighter, I would go out on my bike after tea. One night I met up with Stan Reid, who lived in Shellingford Road, and went to the Holt High School. He had met a girl from Cowley Hill Grammar school, St. Helens. She lived on Broadgreen Road where now the M62 Motorway is built, in a beautiful detached house. Stan introduced her to me and one night we decided to go for a ride on our bikes to Huyton Quarry. We went through Roby and up into Huyton Village, then along

Preparing To Bat, Corwen, August 1945. *Left to right* Len Hunt, unknown, Harry James, unknown, Ken Blasbery, unable to name the other boys.

98

the footpath by Huyton Station, passing Liverpool Girls' College and on into Huyton Quarry. We went down a quiet country lane and decided to sit at the side of the road. We had hardly sat down before we were confronted by an Irishman brandishing a shotgun and shouting at the girl that she was a Hussy and leading us two boys into sin. He ordered us to pick up our bikes and walk in front of him to his farm, about a quarter of a mile away. When we arrived, he ordered the girl into cow shed.

Stan went with her. I plucked up courage and said to him "You can't keep us here, I'm going to the Police Station", I jumped on my bike and pedalled like mad to Huyton Police Station. I Burst into the office gasping out my story to the Sergeant behind the desk. He was very calm and said "Ride back and tell McCarthy to release your friends. If they are not back here within half-an-hour, I will send some of my men to make sure they are safe". I rode back, delivered my message to a now penitent McCarthy who had been harangued by his wife to let Stan and the girl go. They were released without another word and we rode back to the Police Station to report their safe release. We gave Huyton Quarry a wide berth after that.

At College, our 'Wide Boy', named Nickson had an elder brother who knew where to buy American chewing gum, so one afternoon we walked down Park Lane to a little door next to Greenbergs, the Sailors Outfitters. We knocked on the door and it was opened by a little Chinese man who said "Wa you wan". We replied that we wanted to buy American chewing gum. He stood back to allow us to enter a dimly lit passage. At the end there was a small electric light in front of a door. He knocked and a voice said something we didn't understand.

The door was opened to reveal a smoke-filled room with about six Chinese men sitting round a large table. One man, we took to be the leader, said "How you know about Chew Gum"? Nickson replied that his brother had been for some the previous day. 'OK" said the man, "2.6d. for three packs". We hurriedly found our money, the gum was put on the table and we walked out as bravely as we could. This was another place we didn't go back to.

This year's Company Display took place as usual in Tuesday and Thursday, 5th & 7th June in the Church Hall, Dinas Lane. The now familiar programme was performed and I received my second promotion to Corporal.

On 15th June, Family Allowance was introduced, paying 5/- for every child after the first. On 30th July 'The Robinson Family' the first daily Drama serial was broadcast.

In the Summer session at B.B. we would play cricket, baseball and sometimes football. We would prepare for camp by taking out the tents that were stored in the attic of Roby Vicarage, and erect them on the Vicarage lawn. Any repairs that needed attending to were soon done, the requisite number of guy ropes and pegs counted and put away with the tent.

This year we were going to Corwen, a little town close to the River Dee. Our site had the river running along one side, so we were able to have running water for washing both ourselves and our dishes. As usual, we were away for the August Bank Holiday.

At home crowds of people were making for the seaside with New Brighton being very popular. There were cloudless blue skies and glorious sunshine.

We also enjoyed the sunshine. On the Sunday morning we paraded with our band to the Parish church and afterwards marched the length of the main street to the railway station and back again. I was Tent Commander and had as my second in command, Len Hunt. His dad was the Senior Officer, below our Captain "Dickie" Jarvis.

One of my jobs each morning was to go into the town to the paper shop in the little square, where I would buy the newspapers for the officers. I became friendly with the young girl who served behind the counter. Her name was Helen Davies and she had relatives who lived close to my cousin Betty in Liverpool.

Helen had two friends, Mai Jones and Venice Roberts. Mai was friendly with my friend Phil Crossland, who like me was a bugler in the band.

VJ Day Street Party Alderson Road, Liverpool 15, August 1945.

We would meet at night and walk along the main street, talking and laughing and I am sure we were annoying the local boys by being with 'their' girls.

There was a cinema there called the Gwalia. I didn't go, but those who did, said it was not like our comfortable Granada cinema at Dovecot with its plush seats. There, they had benches without cushions and the film would break down several times.

The war in the Far East was coming to an end, with such headlines in the newspapers on 7th August, 'Plan for all out Atomic Attack immediately'. The end of the War in the Far East came on the 14th when Emperor Hirohito ordered all his Commanders to cease active resistance and surrender their arms.

The Allies had earlier dropped two atomic bombs, one on Hiroshima, on the 6th August, killing 75,000 and on the 9th, on Nagasaki killing a further 65,000 people.

As we had a three month holiday from the Art school, I applied to work on a farm camp. These were run by the Ministry of Agriculture and took young people from the age of fifteen to work on the land.

I was accepted for a two week stay at a camp in Northumberland. About a week before I was due to go, a Rail Warrant and travel instruction arrived. I was to travel from Lime Street to Newcastle upon Tyne. There I was to take a local train to Widdrington. The camp itself was in West Chevington, a small village not far from Widdrington. I arrived in Newcastle after a journey of about five hours, to find that my next train was not due to leave for a further three hours. I went on a short tour of Newcastle and found my way down to the River Tyne. I was interested in the trams that ran across the river to Gateshead. I thought about walking across the bridge to Gateshead, but decided that I might not find my was back in time for my train.

On arrival at Widdrington I was joined by other boys from different parts of the country and a large party of boys from the Kings' School, Newcastle. These boys were boarders at the school and were using up some of their holidays like most of us.

When we arrived at Widdrington station we were counted and then we boarded Army lorries for the journey to the camp. We were again counted and given a bed and bedclothes. We were then taken for a meal in the dining room. After dinner we were allowed to play table tennis or read or listen to the radio before turning in for the night at 10 p.m.

As the following day was Sunday, we were allowed to lie in until 7.30 a.m. then it was wash and dress and make your bed before breakfast. The washroom was very cold even in August and the water was a light brown colour. After breakfast we were taken round the camp area and then given a talk about the duties we would be performing during our stay. I was detailed with a party of twenty other boys for duty on an airfield. Our job was to cut and clear the grass around the perimeter track and at the side of the runway The grass we cut was taken away for animal fodder on the neighbouring farms.

In charge of our party were two Land Army girls, Ella and Marjorie. Ella was from Byker, a district of Newcastle. Her dad was tram driver with Newcastle Corporation. She was very down-to-earth and we got on very well with her.

Marjorie was also from Newcastle, but we were not able to find out very much about her background except that she seemed to come from a wealthy family. She seemed more at ease with the boys of Kings' School.

Another job we were given on the airfield was to clear up the spent 20mm cannon shell cartridge cases. They had been fired from the guns on the aircraft when the Armourers had been testing the guns for accuracy. We all made up cartridge case belts with clips we also found. I brought home about fifty cases and clips.

As we were to be away from the camp all day, we would leave after breakfast at 7.30 a.m. taking a packed lunch with us. To get this, we would queue at a little window in the dining room, before parading in the yard waiting for our transport to take us to work.

On the Saturday we worked until noon, then returned to camp

for lunch. Football and cricket was played during the afternoon.

Dinner was at 6 p.m. and at 7 p.m. a lorry came to take us to Widdrington Miners Welfare Hall, where there was a Youth Dance arranged for us. We all went and had a great time with the local girls, much to the resentment of the local lads!

Our second week was very much like the first. The airfield was very large so we had plenty of grass to cut with our scythes, sickles and pitchforks, no mechanisation for us! On our last afternoon we 'staked out' the two girls with the pitchforks and left them whilst we went for a final look around the airfield and the aircraft. When we came back, the girls had freed themselves and took their revenge by making us walk about two miles as they took the lorry that was to take us back to camp right across the airfield.

The morning of our departure, we were paraded before the camp commander. He was like a Head teacher. He thanked us for our efforts during our stay, then called on the members of staff to pay our wages for the two weeks. We all received £3. Then we were given a packed lunch and taken to the station to catch the train for Newcastle and home. There was no direct train to Liverpool, so I travelled to Leeds, where, after another wait, I caught a train for Liverpool and home, arriving at Lime Street about 6pm.

The two weeks had been a very interesting time, but made me appreciate my home and family. I returned to college in September, and by the end of November, I had obtained an Apprenticeship as a Hand Compositor with Messrs Donald Kendall & Sons, 25, Victoria Street, Liverpool 2. I was given one year's grace for my time at Art college, so served six years apprenticeship. My weekly wage was £1 5/- for a 48 hour week.

So ended the six years of war for me. I was able to complete my apprenticeship and over the next fifty years I was able to follow my craft in many places and to meet many famous people, including the Duke of Athol, Lord McCorquodale and his Serene Highness The Aga Khan.